Living in Space

JAMES S. TREFIL

Living in Space

illustrated with photographs

drawings by GLORIA WALTERS

Charles Scribner's Sons | New York

Copyright © 1981 James S. Trefil
Library of Congress Cataloging in Publication Data
Trefil, James S., date   Living in space.
Includes index.
Summary: Discusses technological and human
aspects of the colonization of space as it
may be experienced by future generations.
1. Space colonies—Juvenile literature.
[1. Space colonies] I. Walters, Gloria, ill.
II. Title.
TL795.7.T73   629.44′2   81-14532
ISBN 0-684-17171-6   AACR2

This book is dedicated to the town of
Red Lodge, Montana, where it was written,
and most especially to Irene and to Vern,
who made me feel at home.

Contents

Living in Space

Introduction

This is a book about a great adventure. At the moment it is an adventure of the mind—something we can dream about. It is likely, though, that in your lifetime it will stop being just a dream and start becoming a reality. I am talking about the exploration and colonization of space.

Public awareness of space has diminished in the decade that has elapsed since the Apollo moon landings. At the same time, the commercial utilization of space has blossomed. Semi private corporations have spun webs of communications satellites around the globe that now handle a large part of our long-distance communications. We routinely see live television broadcasts from all parts of the earth, rarely pausing to wonder at the fact that the signals are relayed to us by satellites in orbit. Weather forecasting by satellite has become commonplace, so much so that a television station could now broadcast weather pictures twenty-four hours a day if it so desired.

During your lifetime this process will speed up. The development of the space shuttle will simplify problems associated with construction and maintenance of space structures, and eventually crews of technicians will spend long periods in space, much as isolated crews of workmen now spend long periods in the arctic working on the Alaskan oilfields and pipelines. Eventually, someone will propose that permanent homes be established outside of the atmosphere.

When that happens, the human race will be taking the first step on the road to a destiny that is easy to talk about but hard to conceive: the colonization of the galaxy. But before we get into *that* story, we have to see whether the first step is really possible. In this book, we are going to see what a space colony will be like, how it can be built, and what it will be like to live in one. I hope that after reading about this great adventure, some of you may decide to try to help make this dream of colonization into a reality.

PART I: BUILDING THE COLONY

1 | The Requirements of Life

We tend to take the earth for granted. Since the human race evolved here, it is only natural that the kinds of things we need should be precisely those which the earth provides. But if we are going to start talking about human beings living in space, away from the surface of our planet, then we had better develop a pretty clear idea about what parts of our everyday surroundings are actually necessary for survival and which are pleasant but inessential frills. For example, it is clear that human beings need food, but they can and do survive without beefsteaks and Big Macs. Our space colony will have to supply some kind of nourishment for its inhabitants, then, but it will not have to have enough space to raise cattle. Once we have put together a list of those things that the colonists must have, we will have come a long way toward specifying just what the structure of the colony must be.

One way to make such a list is to imagine going through a typical day, cataloguing the various things that affect us, deciding for each whether it is essential or not and, if it is, exactly how closely the space colony has to reproduce earth-like conditions.

For example, when you get out of bed in the morning, you are breathing. Air is essential for survival, as you can see

3

immediately if you think about what would happen if it were not there. So the colony will clearly have to have a supply of air for the colonists to breathe. And, since there is a limit to how often the same air can be taken into the lungs, there will have to be some sort of purification system to recycle the colony's atmosphere.

But the fact that we need air does not mean that the air we breathe must be the same as that available at sea level on earth. Human beings have lived for thousands of years without any harmful effects on high mountains where the air pressure and oxygen content are considerably lower than at sea level. In addition, experiments on deep-sea habitats have involved long periods in which divers have breathed air with a high helium content. Since human beings have managed to get by with such widely varying air supplies, we can conclude that the amount and composition of the colony's air can be varied within broad limits without any harm being done.

Nevertheless, the earth's atmosphere is one example of something that we need every moment of our lives, but which we have to think about only occasionally. The space colonists, on the other hand, will have to be aware of their air supply from the first stages of design and construction of their home.

Another element in our lives that we take for granted is gravity. When we get out of bed in the morning, we know that the floor is "down" and the ceiling is "up." We live our lives constantly fighting the tug of the earth's gravitational attraction, and very few of us, using our muscles alone, ever get more than a few feet above the surface. In space, however, we know that the predominant sensation will be one of weightlessness. We have all seen enough films of astronauts operating in weightless conditions to understand this. We also know that astronauts have remained in weightless conditions for many months. Doesn't this mean that the familiar feeling of weight is not really essential to human life?

Not exactly. Studies of the astronauts returning from extended missions in orbit show that a rather disturbing process takes place. Calcium is taken from the bones by biological processes during weightlessness at the rate of a few percent per month. It is almost as if the body, sensing that a strong skeleton is no longer needed to combat gravity, decides to use the materials in the bones elsewhere.

Fortunately, the effects of such decalcification have been reversible so far, and the astronauts' bone structures return to normal when they come back to earth. But while weightlessness may be fine for an astronaut on a mission of a few months' duration, a drastic physiological effect like this must be taken as a clear warning sign for permanent human habitations in space. So we will have to add gravity, or something else that can take its place, to the list of essential ingredients of a human environment.

Another aspect of our environment that we take for granted is the effect that the earth's atmosphere has in shielding us from the lethal radiation that rains down from space. There are, in fact, two important kinds of radiation we would have to worry about if we were outside of the atmosphere. The first of these are particles emitted by the sun and other stars. They go by the name of cosmic rays. As it is, the atmosphere does not provide complete protection from such rays, and two or three are going through your body every minute even as you read this book. In fact, about one-third of the radiation that the average American receives from natural sources each year comes from cosmic rays that have filtered through the atmosphere. This is not a large amount of radiation—perhaps as much as a few medical X-rays—but it represents a level of radiation that we know the body can handle.

The second type of harmful radiation is in the form of ultraviolet light from the sun. Again, not all of the ultraviolet is absorbed in the atmosphere; some gets through to cause sunburn in unwary individuals. But it can destroy living systems, which is why it is often used to sterilize hospital equipment, and the colonists will have to be protected from it as well as from cosmic rays. Radiation shielding is obviously necessary on the space colony.

Let us continue through our day. When we get out of bed, we enter a house with a controlled temperature. It may be twenty degrees below zero Fahrenheit outside, but it will probably be between sixty and eighty degrees inside. In fact, if you think of the entire range of temperatures in the universe from absolute zero (456 degrees below Fahrenheit) up

This rather fanciful conception of the interior of a large space colony relies on the premise that the first colonies will be built to duplicate living conditions on earth as closely as possible. The mirrors at the top of the structure will regulate the night-day cycle.

to the temperatures in stars (millions of degrees), there is only a very narrow range in which a human being can survive without some sort of help. Temperatures below fifty degrees Fahrenheit begin to get uncomfortable, as do temperatures above one hundred degrees. And although it is possible to survive outside of this range of temperatures, there seems to be little point in planning to build a habitat that would be excessively uncomfortable. This means that the colony will have to have enough energy to maintain a fairly uniform temperature even though it is in space—for, in space, shaded materials not exposed to direct sunlight will be almost at absolute zero, while the temperature in closed bodies exposed to the sun can soar above the boiling point. The colony will need both heaters and air-conditioners.

The next step in our day is breakfast. It would be very expensive to haul the amount of food and water needed each day by human beings to maintain themselves to a space colony from the surface of the earth. So, the colony will have to supply both of these essentials itself. Water, like air, is a recyclable commodity. It can be used and then recovered from wastes by any number of processes that are well-known today. This means that once the initial water supply is at the colony, only a relatively small amount of water will be needed to make up for losses.

The same is not true of food. The colony will need to have enough space to grow its own food, and this means that an appreciable amount of the available living area will have to be given over to agriculture. The requirement of food self-sufficiency, then, will put strong constraints on how small the colony can be. This will be especially true if a varied diet including fresh meat was to be provided.

After breakfast, our typical day usually has us leaving our homes, which are designed to shelter us as individuals and families, and moving into the larger society. We go to school or to work—activities that will surely exist in some form in a space colony as they do on earth. If you think of all of the infinite variety of activities that humans have engaged in, it is hard to see how any single type of work could be singled out as being absolutely essential, in the sense that air and water are. It is probably true that people must be engaged in some sort of activity to be happy, but it does not seem possible to make a more stringent demand on an individual's working day than this.

With the "need" for work, we enter an entirely new branch of requirements on our space colony. A human being could survive physically without work, but most people would not be happy doing so. In this sense, work for many is a psychological rather than a physical need. There are other needs of this type as well. In our typical day, we are normally working only about half of our waking time. An important use of the rest of the day is in various leisure activities. These might include sports, reading, music, or any number of social encounters with friends and neighbors. Recreational facilities for these sorts of things will make life more pleasant for the colonists. In fact, a good deal of the thought that has gone into the design of space habitats has been directed toward meeting these psychological needs rather than the more basic and simpler physical needs.

One of the aspects of space living that has received the most attention is the psychological need for "elbow room." The first colonies are likely to be fairly small, and the question of overcrowding becomes important. One way of approaching this particular problem is to look at some of the earthbound habitats where people have chosen to spend their lives. In figure 1 we show the average number of square feet available to each person in a number of places of high population density.

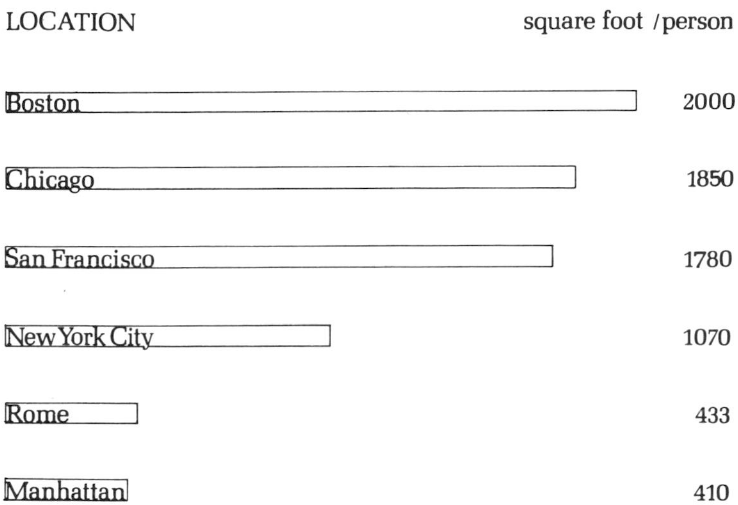

LOCATION	square foot /person
Boston	2000
Chicago	1850
San Francisco	1780
New York City	1070
Rome	433
Manhattan	410

Figure 1

The numbers in figure 1 give us some idea of the amount of space an individual needs to be reasonably happy. There is a wide range of available space in these locations, but all of them share the property of being places where millions of people choose freely to pass their lives right now. Indeed, when I was growing up in Chicago I knew many people who never went outside the city limits in their entire lives, and rarely left their own neighborhood. So when we talk about the number of people who will be living in a space colony, we can be reasonably sure that if the space available per person is in the range of those places shown in the table, there will be no severe problems arising from overcrowding.

A Summary and a Question
We can summarize the discussion thus far as follows: In order for human beings to survive at all, they must have

- a continuous supply of food,
- a continuous but recyclable supply of water and air,
- a regulated temperature,
- gravity near that found on earth,
- protection from cosmic radiation.

In addition, to make life supportable they must have

- useful work,
- living space similar to that on earth,
- leisure and recreational activities.

And now we come to the key question that we will ask in this book:

Is the surface of a planet the only place that these needs can be supplied?

Over the last decade scientists have proposed many ideas about how to answer this question. We will look at some of those ideas in the chapters that follow. They may surprise you.

2 | Designing the Space Colony

The most difficult thing to provide on the list of essentials is gravity. The only known source of gravitational attraction in nature is mass, so to produce something like earth-normal conditions we will have to assemble an object of planetary mass. Since this is beyond any foreseeable technology that we are likely to have, we must provide some sort of artificial effect that will imitate normal gravity. This process we will call the creation of pseudogravity.

There is a familiar form of pseudogravity that we have all experienced. When you are in a train or a fast-moving car and your vehicle goes around a curve, you feel as if you are being pushed toward the outside of the vehicle. This is called the effect of centrifugal force. You may have seen a common carnival ride—the tilt-a-whirl—that operates on the same principle. People stand with their backs against the vertical walls of a large cylinder, which is then rotated. The riders feel themselves pressed against the wall. When the speed is great enough, the floor is pulled down, leaving the riders to enjoy the sensation of being stuck to the wall without any support at all. Again, centrifugal force is at work.

Everyone who has considered the pseudogravity problem has seen the use of centrifugal force as the solution. The idea

11

is that the space station or colony is built in the shape of a sphere or cylinder or doughnut, and then rotated. People inside the colony will then be like the riders of the tilt-a-whirl described above. They will feel the effects of centrifugal force as a pull toward the outside of the structure. This will be "down" as far as they are concerned, and if the size of the structure and the rate of rotation are adjusted properly, the force they feel inside the colony can be made to match exactly the force they would feel on earth.

Let us look at an example to see how this works. The colony shape that seems to be the most efficient at the present time is the doughnut, with the living quarters being inside the "dough." The mathematical term for the doughnut shape is "torus," and since this particular design was first done at Stanford University, this particular type of colony is usually called the "Stanford Torus." In the sketch in figure 2 we show a cutaway view of it.

The torus is rotating about an axis perpendicular to the plane of the colony itself. Consequently, persons standing inside the colony will feel themselves pulled toward the outside by centrifugal force, as shown. Thus, the "wall" of the torus

Figure 2

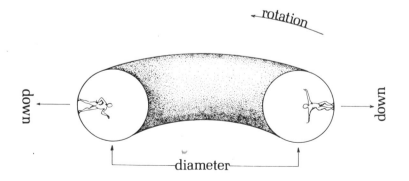

will be the "floor" as far as anyone inside is concerned. If a colonist should drop something, centrifugal force will force it to move outward. The colonist would perceive this as the object moving from the hand to the "floor," and the person would say that when he or she let go of the object, it fell to the "floor." Thus, as far as the colonist is concerned, there is a pseudogravity on the inside of the torus.

For a given size torus, a higher pseudogravity can be produced by spinning the colony faster. For a given rate of spin, a higher pseudogravity can be obtained by making the torus larger. These statements can be translated into a more quantitative form, as in the graph in figure 3, where the solid line represents the requirements for producing normal earth gravity inside the colony. The size of the torus is given by the diameter on the vertical axis (see figure 2). The rate of spin, stated in revolutions per minute, is given on the other axis.

As it turns out, there are important physiological limits to how fast a colony can be spun. The most important of these has to do with something called the Coriolis force, named after Gustav Coriolis, an eighteenth-century French engineer. Perhaps the best way to understand the Coriolis force is to imagine two people standing on the earth—one at the North Pole and the other at the equator. Suppose the person at the pole throws a ball toward his or her partner. While the ball is in the air, traveling southward from the pole, the earth is rotating. Thus, by the time the ball lands at the equator, the person at whom it was aimed will have moved. The ball will not arrive at its intended target.

As far as the people involved in the experiment are concerned, the ball will appear to be deflected while in flight, causing it to fall behind the point at which it was initially aimed. Although we, looking in from the outside, know that the ball traveled in a straight line and the earth moved under-

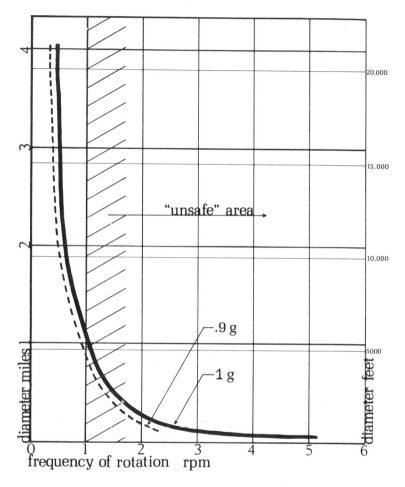

Figure 3

neath it, to people on the earth it looks as if a force acted to deflect the ball away from the experimenter on the equator. This apparent force is called the "Coriolis force" by physicists. It will act whenever something moves in a rotating system. It will, therefore, act in a rotating space colony.

There will be some interesting consequences of this fact in

the colony. For example, if a pitcher throws a baseball at sixty miles per hour—a relatively slow pitch—the Coriolis force in a colony rotating once a minute will cause it to deflect about eight inches by the time it covers the sixty feet between the pitcher's mound and home plate! If the colonists play baseball, there are going to be some fancy pitchers' duels in space.

On a more serious level, there are important systems in the inner ear that are governed by small quantities of moving fluid. These systems control balance. When you get dizzy after spinning around, it is because the fluids in the inner ear have been disturbed. The Coriolis force will act on these fluids as well as on the baseball, and if the rate of spin is too high, anything from mild discomfort to motion sickness to loss of orientation can result. A good deal is known about the effects of rotation on human beings because many agencies, including NASA and the air force, have done extensive testing of pilots. It turns out that the response of the inner ear to rotation is quite small when the rate is as low as three revolutions per minute (rpm), and unmeasurable at one rpm. Consequently, it is generally accepted that for systems such as the space colonies in which human beings will live on a long-term basis, the rotation rate should be no higher than one rpm.

The rate of rotation and the colony size are related to each other. If we take a torus of a given size and spin it faster and faster, the centrifugal force gets bigger and bigger. We could produce any "gravity" we wanted by adjusting the spin. Similarly, if we kept the rate of spin constant and made the torus bigger and bigger, the outer rim would be moving faster and faster and, once more, the pseudogravity would increase. The limit on rotation set by the inner ear is important, therefore, because it tells us something about how big a space colony has to be.

The one rpm limit is shown as a hatched vertical line in figure 3. From the figure, we can immediately see one important fact about space colonies: they have to be big. The smallest colony that can have earth-normal pseudogravity and still rotate at one rpm must be 5,776 feet across—over a mile. Anything smaller than this would have to rotate too fast in order to reproduce earth's gravity. The required size of the colony increases rapidly as the rotation rate drops, going to ten miles for one-third rpm. As a rule of thumb, cutting the rotation rate in half requires the size of the colony to increase by a factor of four.

From this discussion, the reason for the toroidal shape of the space colony is obvious. If the colony has to be a mile across and if people can only live on the outer wall, then it would be a great waste of material to build a cylinder or a sphere, since either of these designs would enclose a lot of empty space. The "hole" in the doughnut is not useful living space, so there is no reason to expend a lot of materials to close it in.

But even the torus requires a great deal of material. For example, if the diameter of the doughnut is 5,776 feet, and if the distance across the living space is 180 feet—a typical design—then to build a one-inch-thick shell around the entire torus would require no fewer than 23,000 tons of aluminum. Estimates for the total amount of material in the Stanford Torus, including atmosphere, run around 150,000 tons. If we compare this to the payload of the first space shuttle—32 tons—we can get some idea of the construction task involved in colony building.

You might think that one way to shrink the colony would be to reduce the level of pseudogravity. It is possible, for example, that future experiments will show that the gravity at the level of 90 percent earth-normal will have no adverse

The interior of a space colony built on the design of the Stanford Torus might look like this. The rotation of the torus will produce earth-like gravity conditions, and the "wall" of the torus will be the "floor" to anyone inside.

physiological effects. Unfortunately, such a finding would not result in a large reduction in the required size of the colony. The dotted curve in figure 3 shows the colony size for 90 percent earth-normal gravity. At one rpm, the diameter of the colony is reduced to 5,479 feet from 5,776 feet—still a little more than a mile. If we wanted to reduce the size of the colony by a factor of two, we would have to accept one-quarter of earth-normal gravity. So it seems as if the twin requirements of normal gravity and a rotation rate of one rpm or less lead inexorably to a structure whose size is measured in miles rather than yards.

The requirements of food, air, and water will be covered in later chapters. It turns out that these are relatively easy to meet. That leaves for discussion only the problem of shielding the colony from cosmic rays.

There are several different aspects of this problem. For one thing, the more energy a cosmic ray has, the harder it is to stop. For another, the rate at which cosmic rays strike the colony will not be constant, but will increase dramatically when the "weather" on the sun produces a solar flare. Finally, just stopping the primary cosmic ray will not be necessarily enough to protect the inhabitants of the colony. When a primary cosmic ray hits the walls of the colony it may stop, but in the process it will produce a spray of lower-energy particles, which, in their effect on tissue, are just as harmful as the original primary ray particles.

There are two mechanisms that protect us from cosmic rays on earth. In the first place, the earth is surrounded by a magnetic field, which deflects the slower particles. More importantly, the earth's atmosphere is a fine absorber of both primaries and secondaries because it is so thick. In fact, there is about a ton of air above each square foot of the earth's surface. Between these two factors, the radiation at sea level is brought down to acceptable levels.

Building a magnetic field around the colony, while possible in principle, would have several drawbacks. In the first place, the small size of the colony would mean that the strength of the magnetic field would have to be quite high to do an adequate job of shielding. This in itself might lead to health problems for the colonists; we are just beginning to study the effect of strong electrical and magnetic fields on living organisms. But from an engineering standpoint the worst aspect of a magnetic shield is that it would not be fail-safe. If something happened and the magnet turned off, the colonists would be exposed to cosmic rays until the shield could be repaired. This is not a pleasant prospect, especially if the breakdown were serious or happened during a solar flare. Consequently, current thinking on this topic favors the use of absorbing materials for the shielding job.

This concept, called passive shielding, is quite simple. Enough material has to be stacked up around the outside of the torus so that both primary and secondary particles are absorbed before they can get to the colonists. In effect, we build an artificial "atmosphere" that cannot be breathed, but that can do the absorption job. The shield will just be a large ring of material sitting stationary in space, while the torus rotates inside of it. Such a system would be fail-safe, simply because nothing short of the destruction of the shield would expose the colonists to dangerous radiation.

The shielding material on earth is air, of course, but it would be impractical to use air for shielding the colony. The colonists will almost certainly use some heavy material for this purpose. Later on, we will see how waste rock and slag could be built up into a radiation shield (see figure 4). With material of this sort, a layer six feet thick would provide as much shielding as does the earth's atmosphere. Unfortunately, a six-foot-thick ring of rock over a mile in diameter

Figure 4

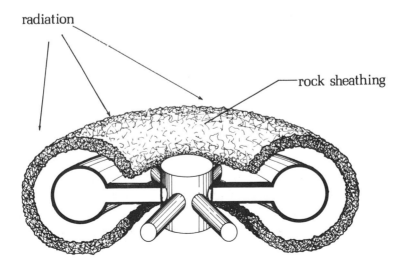

radiation

rock sheathing

would be quite a cumbersome thing. It would weigh no less than 10 *million* tons, as opposed to 150 *thousand* tons for the colony proper. Thus we see that if a passive shielding system were to be adopted, 99 percent of the weight of the colony would be in a ring of inert rock surrounding the living quarters.

The problem of moving this much material into orbit will be discussed in the next chapter, but we should notice that a passive shield of this type would also help to protect against another hazard of space: meteors. One kind of disaster that we usually think about when the subject of space colonies comes up is the collision of a large chunk of rock with the fragile skin of the colony. Actually, the probability of someone in the colony getting hit by something that size is about the same as the probability of someone on earth being killed by a meteor—it is pretty small. It is much more likely that the colony would be hit repeatedly by much smaller bits of space debris—anything from grains of dust on up. In the table below we show the frequency of hits on the Stanford Torus for a variety of sizes of meteoroids, together with the damage caused by each hit.

size	time between hits of this size	equivalent damage
grain of sand	21 days	cap from a toy pistol
pea	58 years	two sticks of dynamite
Volkswagen	1 billion years	200 tons of TNT

From this table it is obvious that the large-scale catastrophe involved in the collision of a large meteor with the colony can safely be ignored. What does have to be considered are the smaller-scale collisions caused by collisions with fast-moving but small bits of space debris. A glance at the "equivalent damage" column in the table shows that these sorts of collisions, though relatively frequent, are capable of causing much less damage than the more catastrophic ones. It is also clear that a six-foot-thick layer of rock around the colony will be capable of absorbing most of the damage caused by the more common meteors.

Summary

The requirements that the colonists experience near earth-normal gravity and at the same time not be subjected to more than one revolution per minute result in a colony that would have to be at least a mile across. The problem of shielding such a large structure from cosmic radiation and from small meteoric debris could be handled by surrounding the structure with a layer of rock about six feet thick. Unfortunately, such a shield would weigh over 10 million tons, and would therefore increase the problem of transporting material to the construction site enormously.

3 | Materials for the Colony and How to Get Them Way Out There

The fact that it is possible in principle to build a home in space does not mean that it can actually be done. There is no guarantee that anything like the mile-long doughnut we described in the last section could be put together in space. In fact, if you think about it for a moment, you will realize that we are talking about putting huge amounts of building materials into orbit for this particular venture.

Take the figure of 150,000 tons for the mass of the Stanford Torus. If we used the first generation of the space shuttle to put this material into near earth orbit, it would take 3,688 trips (at 32 tons per trip). At the projected shuttle capacity of a trip every two weeks, it would take one shuttle 180 years to lift all that material. And this does not include the construction crews or the material needed to keep them healthy during the lifetime of the project.

Even with the improved versions of the shuttle—the so-called heavy lift launch vehicles—that NASA has under consideration, things will not be a whole lot better. These craft have a payload of about five hundred tons, so they would require only three hundred trips to move the colony material off the surface of the earth. But even though we could imagine such vehicles making three hundred trips over a ten-year period, we still have not considered the radiation shield, which would require a thousand times as many takeoffs. This leads us to a second major question about space colonies:

Must the materials for the colony come from the planet earth?

Think of all of the disadvantages of building the colony solely with materials from earth. In the first place, many of the prime structural materials for the colony, such as aluminum, are getting to be scarcer and more expensive on earth. One space colony would not empty our reserves, of course, but because these materials can be used in so many ways right here, it is likely that there would be opposition to loading them on rockets and sending them on a one-way trip into space.

Secondly, every bit of building material taken from earth has to be lifted laboriously and at great cost into orbit. We have to pay an "energy tax" to get materials away from the earth. In addition, each launch must dump some exhaust chemicals into the upper atmosphere. This means that the large number of launches required for a project of this type could cause extensive environmental damage.

Finally, rockets are an extremely wasteful way to transport materials—the fuel that is to be burned near the end of a flight has to be carried along at the beginning, when it is simply dead weight as far as the engines are concerned. This is why the first stages of our current generation of rockets are always so big as compared with the final payloads. The flight would be much more economical if the payload could somehow be accelerated using a power source that did not move along with it, but remained fixed on the ground.

The Energy Tax

From the point of view of gravity, the solar system in the region of the earth resembles a gently sloping hillside dotted with a few narrow but very deep holes (see figure 5). The slope of the hillside has to do with the gravitational attraction that the sun exerts on everything in its vicinity, and the holes correspond to the planets. We are living at the bottom of the gravitational hole corresponding to the planet earth, but the space colonies will be located somewhere up on the hillside. What we have called "paying the energy tax" corresponds to the amount of work we have to do to climb out of the hole, *if* the situation is such that we had to carry all the materials we want to use in space on our backs as we began the climb.

When we think about the energy tax in terms of numbers, it does not look so big. To lift a pound of material from the earth's surface into deep space requires roughly eight kilowatt-hours of energy—about enough to run a window air-conditioner for a day. The reason that rockets designed to

Figure 5

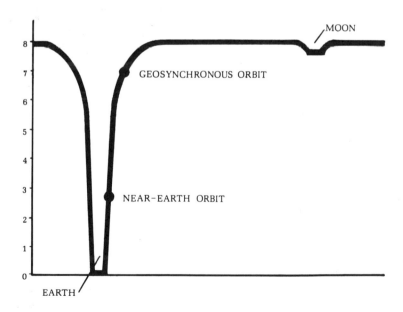

launch satellites are so large is that most of what they lift is fuel, not payload.

It stands to reason that the amount of energy tax that is paid depends on how far out of the hole we want to climb. For example, if we just wanted to put our material in near-earth orbit (a few hundred miles up), we would need four kilowatt-hours of energy per pound, with almost the entire expenditure going into getting the material moving fast enough to keep it in orbit. The farther the orbit is from earth, the more energy we need to put a pound of material into it. As is shown in figure 5, by the time we get out to the so-called geosynchronous orbit—the orbit where the satellite moves just fast enough to appear to stay above one point on earth—it costs a little over seven kilowatt-hours. This is where most communication equipment will be placed in the future. Finally, the full energy tax would have to be paid if we wanted the colony to be in deep space.

Obviously, it would be to our advantage to pay as little energy tax as possible on the materials needed for the colony. But could we pay less than eight kilowatt-hours per pound? We could not if we took our materials from earth, of course, but a glance at figure 5 shows that there is plenty of material around with a much lower energy tax than this. The total tax on a pound of material lifted into deep space from the surface of the moon, for example, is only about one-third of a kilowatt-hour—just a fraction of the tax of earth. So if we could find a way to use lunar materials for the colony, the whole job would be a lot easier. And that is where we come across the cleverest transportation system I have ever seen: the mass driver.

The Mass Driver
The man most identified with the idea of space colonies is a physicist from Princeton University, Gerard O'Neill. It was

he who first pointed out that it is possible to build colonies, and it was he who devised the scheme for transporting materials in space that will make the colonies possible.

To understand the importance of his proposal, let us go back and review what we learned about moving materials into space at the start of this chapter. Rockets were inefficient, we said, because they had to carry their fuel with them. It would be much more economical if we could keep the energy source on the ground and just shoot the materials into space. On earth, for example, something shot out at the speed of seven miles a second—much faster than any bullet—would climb out of the earth's gravitational well without any further help if not for the air resistance it would encounter. This speed is called the "escape velocity" for earth. In many early science-fiction stories, the concept of escape velocity was used to explain spaceships that in the end resembled nothing so much as giant artillery shells. The ships would not have worked, of course, because air resistance would have slowed them down very quickly if it did not burn them up completely.

But there is no air on the moon, and the escape velocity there is a little over a mile and a half per second—much lower than on earth. This means that if we could get something on the moon moving at this speed, it would just go out into space by itself. The only fuel requirement would be whatever was needed to get the object moving at escape velocity in the first place; from then on only the payload would move. So if we could find a way to accelerate things efficiently on the moon, the basic inefficiency of rockets as material movers could be overcome.

Of course, it is one thing to comment that it would be nice to have something, and quite another to come up with a scheme to build it. O'Neill realized this when he first proposed the idea of the space colony, and he devoted a good part of his considerable talents to coming up with a practical design for the kind of transport system we have just described. The concept that resulted from his work is the "mass driver."

Let us suppose we had a pile of material we wanted to send out into space from the surface of the moon. If we were using a mass driver, the first thing we would do is break the pile up and pack it into bundles about the size of a loaf of French bread—four inches across and less than two feet long. We would put these into a container whose outside dimensions are about the size of a garbage can. This container is called the "bucket," and it is the heart of the mass driver. There is a great deal of machinery in it, and that is why its

The four large horizontal cylinders in this artist's concept of a lunar base contain the base habitat, maintenance facility, soil-packaging plant, and loading facility for the mass driver, the long tube-like structure extending to the horizon. The solar cell array on the left will be used to power the base and the mass driver.

inside carrying space will barely accommodate the small payload while its outside diameter is so big. The bucket and payload are then put into the mass driver itself, which will be simply an open tube several miles long. In this tube the bucket is accelerated up to escape velocity and then, at the last minute, the bucket is stopped. At this point the payload flies out of the front end of the bucket, which has been left open for exactly this purpose. The payload continues on its way, having been given escape velocity. The bucket is then returned to the loading platform, where it picks up another bundle and repeats the entire process.

The details of the acceleration process are not difficult to understand. They use well-known scientific principles, which are applied, however, in a novel way. No scientific breakthrough is needed to make the mass driver work—just a concerted effort to develop the design and make it more efficient.

The inside of the bucket contains a large magnet. This magnet is made of superconducting material—materials that can carry electrical currents with no loss of energy, provided that they are kept at temperatures near absolute zero. A superconducting magnet is just a coil of wire made from such material. At some point it is connected up to a battery or other electrical source and a current is run through it. Then the battery is disconnected and the current continues to flow. In principle it will flow forever. The current creates a magnetic field just as an ordinary bar magnet would, so this sort of device is just a very efficient way of making a magnet. Superconducting magnets have many industrial and scientific applications and, in fact, there are many companies around the world that manufacture them routinely.

To keep the magnets superconducting, the inside of the bucket has to be filled with liquid helium, a substance that exists at a few degrees above absolute zero. This accounts for the bucket's bulk. But once the bucket has been magnetized, the rest of the acceleration process can go on.

The first thing that happens is that the bucket is levitated. Most of us are familiar with the fact that we can make one small magnet move by bringing another magnet near it. If we set the magnets up so that the north pole of one is near the south pole of the other, they will move toward one another. If we set them up so that the two north poles, or the two south poles, are near each other, they will be repelled from each other. Now, the bucket is just a big magnet, and therefore it, too, has a north and a south pole. If we put the bucket above another magnet in such a way that the north pole of the bucket is above the north pole of the other magnet, and if the strength of the other magnet is high enough, then the repulsion between the two magnets could be strong enough to overcome the force of gravity on the bucket and the bucket would not fall. It would literally be levitated by the magnetic force.

In the long accelerating track of the mass driver, electrical currents flow in a metal bed so that the north pole of a magnet always appears under the bucket. The bucket "floats." Since there is no air on the moon, this means that there is nothing to slow the bucket down—no friction at all. This ideal condition can never be achieved on earth without complicated and expensive vacuum systems, which is yet another reason why the surface of the moon is a good place to build the mass driver.

The actual acceleration of the floating bucket will probably be done by running electrical current through wires on the outside of the tube. The current will be timed in such a way that it pulls the bucket along with it. Again, this is a well-known technique and is already being used extensively in many ways on earth. The bucket will spend about three seconds being pulled up to lunar escape velocity, during which time it will travel almost two miles. At this point the bucket will be jerked out from under the payload, and the payload will move off across the lunar surface in a straight line.

The actual aiming of the bucket and payload will require some fancy electronics, but nothing that cannot be handled easily by good engineers today. There will probably be several final aiming stations to make last-minute corrections in direction, and then the payload will move away from the moon, gradually rising above the lunar surface, and then, a few days later, arriving at the collection point forty thousand miles away in space.

The collector will be a large cone-shaped ship, dubbed the "catcher's mitt in space," with its large open end pointed toward the stream of bundles coming up from the mass driver. When it is full it will trundle off to the building site, leaving the collection to a sister ship. In this sense, the collectors would be like modern ocean-going ore carriers plying the seas between mines and factories.

In the last few years two research groups—one led by O'Neill and one at Los Alamos Laboratories in New Mexico—have been developing ways of accelerating payloads using electrical systems. In recent experiments small cubes of plastic (perhaps an inch on a side) have been accelerated to speeds of almost ten miles per second. This is about the escape velocity from earth, and is considerably higher than the escape velocity from the moon.

Consequences of Lunar Mining

With the mass driver, then, we have a system that is capable of delivering large quantities of materials from the moon to a construction point in space. Most of these materials would simply be scraped from the surface of the moon by the lunar equivalent of bulldozers and packaged into payloads.

But there is one important consequence of lunar mining that will appear again and again in our discussions from this point on. If the colony is to be built with materials taken from the moon with a minimum of transportation originating on earth itself, then we must realize that these would be very different from common materials we are used to. Many Americans live in wood houses because the North American continent is still heavily forested and wood is relatively inexpensive and plentiful. Desert dwellers live in adobe or rock houses because clay and rocks are cheap and plentiful where they live.

In the same way, the colonists in space will have to build and grow used to those materials that are easiest for them to acquire. In their case, these will be those materials most common on the surface of the moon near the mass driver. In the next chapter we will discuss the consequences of this fact as far as the structural part of the colony goes, but it is important to accept that wooden furniture is likely to be pretty rare in space, along with many other materials that we are used to. In addition to wood, things like leather, silk, cotton, and other natural materials will simply disappear from the human scene.

4 | Building in Space

There are two problems that must be addressed if we want to talk about building space colonies with materials gathered on the moon. The first question is: *What kinds of building materials will we have and how can they be obtained from ordinary lunar soil?* The second is: *How, once the basic materials are available, can we put the colony together?*

From Moon Rock to Metal

As it happens, we know a good deal about the surface of the moon because of the study of the moon rocks brought back by the Apollo astronauts. We know, for example that the material at the lunar surface is not hard rock for the most part, but a fine powder. The small grains of powder tend to stick together at the points where they touch each other. So, you can think of the lunar surface as being made of something like a microscopic popcorn ball. This means that moving the material around in a mining operation would be much easier than a similar operation on earth—one lunar scientist compared it to digging in face powder. The energy expenditure in taking the materials from the surface of the moon to the mass driver entrance, then, would be quite small.

There are some important facts about lunar materials that bear on the building of colonies. The first is that the Apollo samples were surprisingly rich in ores containing aluminum and titanium—two prime structural materials. They are also rich in oxygen, so that we could expect the process of extracting the metals from their ores to produce enough of this vital substance to supply the colony with its air, with enough left over to use as a rocket propellant as well. The greatest problem the builders will encounter is the lack of both water and hydrogen on the moon. There is, so far as we know, no free water there at all, although some geologists have suggested that there might be some under the surface. Water is made from hydrogen and oxygen, and although the latter is fairly common on the moon, the former is not. In fact, there is no place on the surface of the earth that has less hydrogen than does the surface of the moon. This means that when engineering starts on the moon and in space, water will have to be very carefully recovered and recycled. It will be much too precious to waste.

The types of ores found on the moon are also found on the earth, but they are not mined at present because there are other ores here that are more economical to use. For example, aluminum on the moon is found in something called anorthosite ores, while on earth it is found in bauxite. The latter is a relatively simple mixture of aluminum, oxygen, and bound water, while the former is a more complex mixture of sodium, silicon, oxygen, and aluminum. As high-grade aluminum ores on earth are being used up, research is already starting on ways of extracting aluminum from earthly anorthosites. The Bureau of Mines has developed processes by which this can be done, although the cost is still too high for the new process to compete with the older methods of getting aluminum from bauxite. Nevertheless, the simple fact that research on this problem is underway means that the actual extraction of metals from lunar soil will not present insurmountable difficulties when the time comes to build the colonies.

But it is important to realize that we cannot just take a metallurgical process that works on earth and assume that it will work on the moon or in space. Every process on the earth is carried out in the presence of an atmosphere and gravity. We can look at two examples to see how the absence of either of these will create problems for engineers.

We have already mentioned the fact that the tiny grains of soil in the lunar surface tend to stick together. This happens because of the absence of an atmosphere. This means that even a simple mining operation like grinding up rocks will run into trouble on the moon, because the small grains that result from the grinding will also tend to stick together. On earth, this is not a problem.

In addition, many chemical techniques used on earth use a process called "precipitation." In this process chemicals interact in a liquid to form a solid, which then falls to the bottom of the reaction vessel. But in the zero-gravity conditions of space, the solid would not separate from the liquid— it would just keep floating around. In space manufacturing processes, then, any precipitation technique would have to be carried out in a centrifuge, where the pseudogravity supplied by the rotation would separate the solid from the liquid.

These are just two examples of the kinds of problems engineers are likely to encounter in their new environment in space. They are not insurmountable problems by any means, but they do show that it will not be possible to take techniques that work well on earth into the space environment *in toto*. In this sense, engineering in space is no different from engineering in any other new set of surroundings. The deep ocean floor and the arctic oil fields are two less exotic places where new and difficult engineering problems had to be solved before meaningful exploitation of resources could take place.

But you should not get the idea that space presents only problems to the engineer. In fact, it possesses one abundant resource that more than makes up for any problems that might exist. That resource is sunlight. In space the sun shines twenty-four hours a day, and it is not dimmed by an atmosphere. The solar energy is there for the taking. For metallurgy, this means that processes that are energy-intensive, and therefore expensive, on earth can be carried out quite easily. For example, most of the techniques that have been proposed for extracting metals from lunar ores begin by melting the ores in a large container. The heat required for melting comes from a series of mirrors that concentrate sunlight on the ore, raising its temperature. The molten ore is then processed chemically to extract the metal.

The same melting process can be used to extract another common and useful material from lunar soil: silicon. Silicon, which is the main component of ordinary beach sand, is the material used to make solar cells. These cells convert sunlight directly into electricity, and they are already widely used in satellites and ground-based solar energy systems. They will probably be used to supply the electricity for the construction and operation of the space colony as well, so it is fortunate that they can be built easily with lunar materials.

In addition to pure silicon, the same processes that yield aluminum and titanium will produce, as a by-product, the basic materials for making many different kinds of glass and ceramics. In fact, the space factories will produce things like fiberglass in great quantities, so that this material, which is used already in making everything from containers to sailboats on earth, will be another common building material in space.

Finally, we should note that hydrogen, the scarcest material on the moon, is not completely absent from the ores that would be processed in the space factories. Even though there is no native hydrogen on the lunar surface, we know that there is a constant rain of cosmic rays falling on it. Most of these cosmic ray particles are protons, the nuclei of hydrogen atoms. When these protons hit the moon, they are absorbed into the powder they encounter at the surface. They pick up stray electrons and become ordinary hydrogen atoms. Although this is a slow process and the density of cosmic rays is very low, over the 4.5 billion years that the moon has been around, a certain small concentration of hydrogen has accumulated. This hydrogen would be given off by the ores as they were heated and could easily be recovered at the space factory.

The 10 million tons of material needed to build the space colony could be expected to yield about four hundred tons of hydrogen. This can be burned with the oxygen we talked about above to produce heat—always a useful commodity in an industrial operation—and water. In the process the four hundred tons of hydrogen would become thirty-six hundred tons of water—about ninety thousand gallons, or enough to fill a dozen large swimming pools. This would go a long way toward supplying the colony's water, but the rest would either have to be made from hydrogen brought up from earth or hydrogen baked out of lunar soil on the moon itself. In either case, so long as we depend on the moon for our supplies, water will be both scarce and expensive. One estimate puts its cost at fifty dollars per gallon—about the cost of a good wine or Scotch whiskey. But unlike the wine and whiskey, the water will be recycled and used many times.

We can summarize results of this survey of lunar resources in the following way:

1. There are sufficient resources on the lunar surface to allow us to obtain material for the colony, but we may have to develop new techniques for refining lunar ores.
2. Aluminum, titanium, and various glasses and ceramics will be available in abundance for building. Silicon for solar cells and oxygen for breathing and for rocket fuel will also be easy to get.
3. Hydrogen will be the scarcest and most valuable commodity in the colony, and a good deal of the colony's supply will have to come from earth.

The Actual Construction

The absence of strong gravitational forces in space may be a nuisance as far as refining ores is concerned, but it will be a great help when the time comes to start putting the colony together. On earth, structures have to be very large just so they can support their own weight. Think of a bridge like the Golden Gate in San Francisco, with a central span of over four thousand feet. It is a huge structure made of steel and concrete. It has to be huge because anything smaller would collapse of its own weight. But if there were no gravity and no weight, all that steel and concrete would not be needed. A light aluminum girder could be stretched from one shore to the other, and, because it would be in a weightless environment, it would not buckle or sag.

This is the great advantage of building in space. The zero-gravity conditions means that structures of stupendous size can be erected with relatively small quantities of building materials. For example, in a later chapter we will talk about solar power satellites—satellites designed to generate power

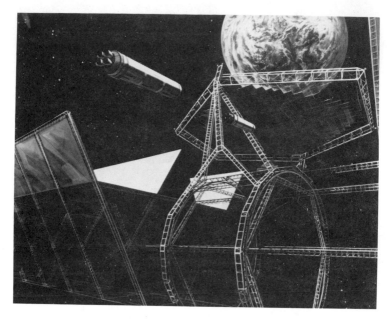

Solar power satellite systems, such as this artist's concept of one with an orbital transfer vehicle, will initiate large-scale construction in space, creating experience in space construction that will prove valuable when people start to think seriously about building colonies.

in space and beam it back to earth. The design that people are talking about would intercept enough sunlight to replace five nuclear reactors or coal plants. To do this, the structure would have to be almost 9 *miles* long and 3.5 *miles* wide. On earth, a self-supporting structure of this size would require huge amounts of materials, yet the total mass of the satellite system is only twenty thousand tons. For reference, this is the amount of steel it would take to fill a cube about fifteen yards on a side. The reason the solar power satellite can be so large is that it can be built with hollow triangular girders made of aluminum.

Solar power satellites will probably be built within the next twenty years, simply because they are a relatively pollution-free way to generate electricity and cost no more than coal or nuclear energy. This means that by the time people start to think seriously about building colonies, they will have had a good deal of experience with putting together large structures in space. In fact, the dimensions of the colony are small compared to those of even a single power satellite.

The leading proponent of the solar satellite concept is Dr. Peter Glaser of the Arthur D. Little Corporation. His company has started development of a machine that solves an important problem in space construction. It is a compact machine that takes rolls of aluminum several inches wide and turns out girders of the type discussed above. With this machine, two men working in space can produce girders as long as the Golden Gate bridge in a matter of hours. So even now, with the shuttle era just beginning, the equipment for large-scale construction in space is being built.

From this, we see that putting together large-scale solar collectors and mirrors around the colony will not be too difficult. But what about the colony itself? Even though it is in space it will have to withstand the forces of pseudogravity associated with rotation. The walls of the main ring of the colony, then, will have to be reasonably strong. This is one reason why the mass of the colony (150,000 tons) is so much greater than that of a power satellite, even though the satellite is so much larger than the colony.

But it turns out that, even for a large construction project like this, the zero-gravity vacuum of space allows us to build in novel ways. Instead of building a skeleton for the colony from metal girders and then fastening the outer skin to the skeleton, we can build the outer frame in one piece by using a technique called "vacuum vapor deposition," or VVD (see figure 6).

The way VVD works is quite simple. First a sample of metal in a closed container is heated until it melts, and then

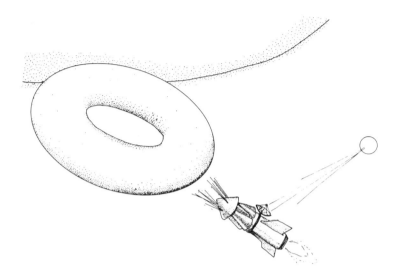

Figure 6

the molten metal is heated until it vaporizes. This process is analagous to boiling water to produce steam. Vaporizing metal requires a lot of energy, of course, but we have already seen that energy in the form of sunlight will be cheap in space. When the vapor has reached the desired temperature, a small hole in the container is opened and the vapor is allowed to come out, just as steam comes from the spout of a kettle. If this were being done in air, the vapor would come into contact with the air, cool, and fall out in a rain of tiny chunks of metal. In the vacuum of space, however, the vapor will move until it comes into contact with a solid surface, at which point it will solidify into a thin layer of metal. So metal can be plated onto a solid surface in a process very similar to using paint from a spray can. Processes similar to VVD are already being used on earth to make high-quality mirrors by plating thin layers of silver and other metals onto solid surfaces.

The construction of the outer hull of the colony, then, could proceed something like this: a large doughnut-shaped balloon is inflated. Then a series of VVD devices move around the balloon, spraying aluminum onto its surface. This aluminum, of course, is the end product of the lunar mining/mass-driver/space-refining process that we have already discussed. The spraying goes on until the wall has reached the desired thickness. The balloon is then deflated, the air being stored for later use, and *voilà*—a single, seamless toroidal hull.

The same process can be used to put together any other closed structures that might be needed in the colony. As we shall see later, a complete colony might well include some small rotating cylinders, separate from the main ring, for growing food. It might include factories and industrial sites that are separate as well. Each of these minicolonies could be put together by following the same steps we have described for the main ring.

To sum up, then, there will be two kinds of structures in space. There will be large zero-gravity mirrors and solar collectors built from a fragile webbing of aluminum girders and incapable of supporting heavy loads. There will also be relatively strong enclosed structures, like the main ring of the colony, capable of retaining an atmosphere and withstanding the forces of pseudogravity. These will be built by vacuum vapor deposition. Once again, we find that present technology gives us a pretty good idea of how things will be done in space.

5 | Three Possible Scenarios
for the Colony

It is one thing to see that building space colonies is within our grasp technically. It is quite another to say that we will decide to build them. Since the Apollo program, public awareness of and interest in space has fallen off dramatically. We can imagine governments in the future too involved with problems at home to invest even the small amount of resources needed to follow the trail that the astronauts have opened. I think, however, that it is almost inevitable that in the lifetime of most readers there will be human beings living permanently in space. In this chapter I give three scenarios as to how this could come about. I list them in order of my personal preference, the most desirable being first.

The Orderly Exploitation of Space

In the late 1950s the first primitive communications satellites were launched by the United States. Little more than inflated balloons capable of reflecting radio waves, they nonetheless revolutionized communications on earth. In the early and mid 1960s, live television broadcasts of exceptional overseas events, such as the Olympics or the crowning of a pope, were available in the United States. They were so exceptional that whenever a satellite broadcast was being aired, a small legend stating "live via satellite" or the equivalent was seen at the bottom of the television screen. Today intercontinental television is so commonplace that we rarely give a thought to the fact that on a typical afternoon we can see football from the United States, skiing from Austria and soccer from Argentina on the same program, all live.

At the same time, more and more commercial and military communication is being routed through the satellite network, from ordinary long-distance phone calls to shipping information. So, at the same time that public interest in space has dropped, public dependence on space has increased dramatically.

With the coming of the shuttle era, exploitation of space will continue to accelerate. Instead of littering space with small satellites, each performing its own specialized mission, platforms several hundred yards on a side will be built to carry arrays of communications equipment. Other platforms will carry equipment to monitor weather and to carry out agricultural and geological analysis. There are even plans to orbit receivers the size of football fields to receive and retransmit signals from radios so small that they can be worn like a wristwatch. The "two-way wrist radio" used in fiction by Dick Tracy may soon be a reality.

So even if we can find no new ways to utilize satellites in the next ten years—a dubious proposition at best—the simple fact that it is easier to maintain and service equipment that is concentrated rather than scattered about means that we will soon develop the ability to put up structures in space that are large by present standards. The structures will still be small, of course, compared to space colonies.

At the same time that this expansion and consolidation of space communication systems is taking place, the energy squeeze will be continuing on earth. The environmental and

The Columbia, the first space shuttle vehicle to fly in space, is the forerunner of future versions of the space shuttle, which will haul materials for the first few solar satellites into near-earth orbit.

safety problems associated with coal and nuclear-generated electricity will continue to make it difficult to meet growing demand, while the growing shortage of petroleum will spur the development of electric cars. Thus, we will have a paradoxical situation in which we will have to generate more electrical energy to conserve our stocks of petroleum energy. At this point, the solar power satellite will become an important part of our energy picture.

The development of these satellites is already underway, and serious design studies have already been done. We will describe them in detail later, but for our present purposes we simply note that they are large structures in space whose purpose is to convert sunlight into electricity and then beam the energy back to earth in the form of microwaves. One large satellite would replace five large-scale coal or nuclear power stations. By the year 2000, we can expect that the pilot plants in this system will have been completed and the construction of the first full-scale system will be underway.

The materials for the first few solar satellites will be hauled into near-earth orbit by improved versions of the space shuttle. With a five-hundred-ton payload, these ships would require about forty trips to put the entire twenty thousand tons of the satellite into orbit. After the structure is assembled it will be towed to a geosynchronous orbit—twenty-three thousand miles from the earth—by a space tug. This will be an expensive process, but the electricity produced will be competitive with that derived from other sources.

In all likelihood the solar power satellite system will be run by a company made up of private corporations and governments. This organization will be analagous to Intelsat, the corporation that now controls communications satellites. After the first full-scale power satellites prove to be moneymakers, as the first communications satellites have, the board of directors will meet to decide on how to go about building more of them.

At this meeting, I expect that the chief engineer will show up with blueprints of a mass driver. He will argue that instead of draining materials from the earth and spending all of that money on rocket launches each time a satellite is built, it would be much more economical to invest once in a lunar mining operation capable of delivering raw materials to a space manufacturing center. The time has come, he will argue, to quit pussyfooting around and go full steam ahead on building power stations in space.

So the mass drivers will be built, not because of an idealistic commitment to the expansion of the human race into space, but because of the plain nuts-and-bolt needs of engineers to have a source of materials for their power stations. The first space factories will be pretty austere places, more analagous to a logging camp or an arctic oil rig than to the colonies we will discuss later. The men and women living in space will be there for short periods of time—perhaps up to a year—and will be drawn by the high pay, the adventure, and the opportunities for advancement that they see there. In this respect the first spacemen will be like any other kind of pioneers. They will be concentrating on the job to be done and not on building a permanent home.

After this sort of thing has been going on for a while, the corporation will start exploring other types of manufacturing processes in space, perhaps setting up permanent factories for manufacturing pharmaceuticals and new materials or for mining asteroids. We will discuss these possibilities later, but we mention them here to show that the space environment may offer commercial advantages besides energy. In any case, as the adventure of work in space wears off, it will become harder to convince people to leave their families and live in the relatively spartan accommodations associated with the power satellites and space factories.

Then, at another meeting of the board, the chief engineer, perhaps aided by the personnel manager, will make another presentation. Once again the main arguments will be economic ones. "The manpower requirements for the growing space industries are just getting to be too hard to meet with short-term workers. We need to build a home in space where families can live while they build the power satellites and carry out other industrial jobs.'' This sort of situation has been encountered before, when mines in remote areas had to be worked. The answer in that case was the company town— an entire town built by the mining company to house its workers. The economics of the two situations—mines and space factories—are pretty similar, and the chances are that the board will go ahead with the proposal to divert a portion of the lunar mining and space manufacturing facilities that they have developed to the building of a space colony to house their employees.

Once again, the building of the space colony will not be the result of dreamy idealism, but of simple economics. This doesn't mean that the colonies will be the kind of dreary place that so many mining towns were. The men and women working in space are likely to be highly skilled technicians and scientists—the kind who are in demand in almost any industry. To attract them, the corporation will have to provide many amenities, not the least of which will be attractive living space. This means that the type of colony we will be describing in the rest of the book, with its emphasis on high-quality living and ample recreational area, is really much more likely to be built than you might think at first.

The Soft Path to Space Colonies
Let us consider another possible future. The shuttle era ushers in the same consolidation of satellite systems that we discussed above, so that some limited ability in the field of space exploration is developed. Earthbound civilizations, however, manage to solve their energy problems without building power satellites. This will be accomplished by an

increased dependence on ground-based solar energy and on increasing exploitation of coal and nuclear energy. General energy use will be lowered, as will the overall standard of living. Nevertheless, societies will survive, more or less in their present form, without power satellites and the exploitation of space will be confined to the web of satellites of the type we have already discussed.

But energy is not the only thing that future societies will have to worry about. Even when the energy crisis has been solved in one way or another, other crises will soon surface. The fact of the matter is that easily recovered supplies of many minerals, from chromium to aluminum, are also being used up rapidly. By the turn of the century we may well look back with nostalgia to the good old days when the only thing in short supply was petroleum.

At this point, people concerned with the resource shortages developing on earth will notice the truly stupendous resources available in space. Depending on what is needed, attention will focus on either the lunar surface or on asteroids whose orbits bring them close to the earth. Asteroid mining is another topic we will talk about in more detail later, but for the purposes of this discussion we will just say that there are many asteroids, several miles across in size, whose orbits bring them sufficiently close to the earth for us to consider extracting valuable minerals from them.

So the scramble for space resources will be on. But instead of the orderly progression we talked about in our first scenario, this will be more like the panicky reaction of the United States to the petroleum shortage. Large sums of money will suddenly be poured into space exploration, without enough prior planning to guarantee that all of the money is spent wisely. In this respect it will resemble the synthetic fuel program going on in the United States today. Nevertheless, like the synfuel program, space exploitation will ultimately work. The first space miners will probably just haul an asteroid rich in needed minerals to the vicinity of the earth, chop it up, and then let the pieces fall into desert areas where they can be recovered and refined. Later, the kind of metallurgical industry we talked about in the last chapter will be set up in orbit.

From this point on, the procession of events will be pretty much like the one we talked about earlier. The space colony will be built as a company town to house people engaged in asteroid (or lunar) mining and processing. The primary difference between these two paths to the space colony is that the first, being an orderly progression, is likely to be more cost-efficient than the second, which involves a panicky response to resource shortages. Nevertheless, the end result of the two paths is the same. Early in the next century, thousands of human beings will likely be living in space on a permanent basis.

The Military Path

War in space has been the subject of so much science-fiction that it scarcely needs to be explained in detail. The possibility that the first space colonies might be military in character has largely been overlooked by writers on the subject, yet it is easy to see how such a state of affairs could arise. And although most of us would probably regard this as the least desirable way for man to move into space, it has to be explored. After all, we have to remember that in the settling of the western United States the first European habitations in many areas were forts.

It might go something like this: During the consolidation and expansion of orbital communications systems in the postshuttle era, a parallel process is taking place in the military satellite system. The "spy-in-the-sky" satellites that both the United States and the Soviet Union maintain are now an integral part of both countries' intelligence systems.

Just as the military and intelligence communities have put up their own intelligence and communications satellites, following closely on those being launched by civilian groups, they can be expected to continue doing so in the future. In addition, military research will soon turn up new kinds of weapons adapted to use in space. The weapons utilizing beams of high-energy particles now being discussed in the United States, and presumably in the Soviet Union, would probably become the prime tool for destroying satellites. Thus we would have a situation where the intelligence system of each nation, vital in the age of the nuclear deterrent, becomes vulnerable to space-based weaponry.

It does not take much imagination to anticipate the responses of the superpowers to this sort of situation. Whatever treaty provisions exist now to keep weapons out of space will be ignored in the face of the threat, be it real or imagined. A steadily escalating buildup of military force in space will follow. First there will be killer satellites to destroy the enemy's communication and intelligence systems, then killer satellite hunters to counter the enemy's killer satellites. The situation will quickly become analagous to that which prevails in the oceans of the earth today, where attack submarines armed with nuclear missiles cruise about, hunted by killer submarines whose mission in wartime will be to destroy them before the missiles can be launched.

Despite the advances in electronics that can be expected to occur in the next few decades, it is unlikely that space weapons will be automatic or controlled from the ground. Long-distance communications would be too vulnerable in time of war. Consequently, the weapons systems would have to be manned. The crews will be selected men, probably not too different from those who now man nuclear submarines. They will stay in space for relatively short times—certainly no longer than a year. Nevertheless, some sort of "home" will have to be provided for them, so the end result of the military move into space will be the construction of space habitations.

However, it is important to realize that the kinds of restrictions we placed on the space colonies in Chapter 2 had to do with the health of people who would live in them for long periods of time. Most of these restrictions could probably be relaxed for shorter-term occupancy by military personnel. For example, it is quite likely that lower gravity requirements could be applied in this case, or that crews could be chosen for their ability to withstand the effects of rapid rotation. Thus the military space dwellings could probably be a good deal smaller than the mile-wide torus we have talked about. Similarly, the absence of families and the crew's knowledge that they would soon be returning to earth would mean that relatively little effort would have to be made to provide a homelike setting. All in all, the military habitat would probably bear as much resemblance to the kind of space colony we are thinking about as a warship does to a luxury liner.

Summary
By far the most attractive road to the future is the first one we described, in which the progression from communications systems to power satellites to space manufacturing to permanent colonies follows an orderly, well-planned progression. The point of the other two scenarios was to show that the orderly exploitation of space is not the only path that will lead to space colonies. In fact, it is difficult to imagine a future in which the living standards of people on earth con-

tinue to rise that does not involve some exploitation of the mineral resources of space.

This does not mean that the existence of space colonies is inevitable, however. One can imagine many futures in which they do not exist. A major nuclear war, for example, could set us back to the point where the human presence in space will simply cease. So could a conscious decision on the parts of all nations to reduce our population to a level that can be maintained on renewable resources only, turning the earth into a pastoral place with very little high technology. I do not consider this a likely option, since it would require that everyone cooperate in this decision. Given our past history of performance in the area of international cooperation, it seems that the prospects for cooperation on a change this massive would be pretty dim. And a decision to move to this sort of future by a single nation or group of nations would simply mean that that particular group had dealt itself out of a future in space, leaving other nations to fill the gap. From the discussion of the military scenario, we see that the advantages of a military position in space are great enough to make a national decision to forgo the development of space tantamount to a policy of unilateral disarmament—never a popular course of action.

PART II: LIFE IN THE COLONY

6 | Home Sweet Home

The physical facts that we have discovered about the space colony—that it will be a mile across, for example, or made of aluminum—do not tell us everything about what the colony would be like. The fact that people *can* live in such a place still leaves a lot of leeway in the details of *how* they will live. For example, people in the colony will certainly have homes, but the homes will not necessarily be made in the same way as those back on earth. As it turns out, however, once we know how the colony will be built we can make a pretty good guess as to what the living conditions there will be.

In the first place, we know how much space there will be. In the Stanford Torus, a mile across and 180 feet wide, there will be a little over four hundred acres of available "ground" area. Depending on the details of the design of the colony, a community of ten thousand souls would then have between 450 and 500 square feet available per person. This is the equivalent to room a little over 20 feet on a side—a moderately large living room or a small classroom.

In Chapter 1 we discussed the human need for living space and showed the amount of space available in a number of major cities (see figure 1). Referring back to that figure, we

VILLAGE

HUB

TUBE

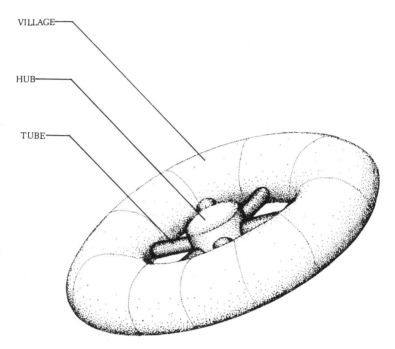

Figure 7

see that the colony will actually have more living space per person than Manhattan and Rome, two locations that are usually considered desirable. It will certainly not be as crowded as Hong Kong, which packs a human being into every 100 square feet. So the vision of the space colony as some sort of rabbit warren with people crowded into every available nook is clearly wrong. The structure will be large enough to give the architect leeway in the use of "land" area.

On the other hand, the colony will be no place for people who need lots of elbow room all of the time. The spacious suburban home surrounded by a private lawn—the ideal so cherished in America today—will clearly not be available in the colony. The designs that have been done so far call for grouping the dwellings together into the space equivalent of clusters of high-rise apartment buildings, with open areas left in between. This is the sort of design used by most advanced city planners on the earth today, and it seems to work well. Communities such as Reston, near Washington D.C. that are designed to group houses together in little "villages" surrounded by open spaces seem to be considered pleasant places to live. Old farming towns in France and Italy operate on the same principle and have served as dwellings for tens of generations of human beings. There is no reason why the best of this design experience should not be applied in space.

One way such a system might work is shown in figure 7, where we give a top view of the Stanford Torus in a little more detail than we have up to this point. The main ring is divided by six tubes, which more or less play the role of spokes in a wheel by connecting to a central hub. The hub is four hundred feet across and the tubes fifty. The idea is to locate a cluster of buildings at the end of the spokes in each tube. These clusters would be villages of less than two thousand people each. Designers have given them fanciful names like "Vail" and "Ventura," but my guess is that the colonists will give them names more suited to the new adventure in space. But in any case, if you lived in one village and wanted to visit a friend in another, you would have two choices. You could either walk or ride around the ring through the open spaces between villages, or you could go through the tubes. If you chose to walk, it would not take you long. Remember that the ring is less than four miles around, so no part is more than half an hour's walk from any other.

If you chose to use the tubes, however, the trip would be an object lesson in the nature of the pseudogravity generated by centrifugal force. You would board an elevator at the foot of one of the tubes and start "up" toward the hub. As the elevator moved in the tube, you would begin getting lighter.

Halfway to the center you would weigh only one-fourth of what you did at the rim. By the time you reached the edge of the central hub you would be almost weightless. For example, someone starting the trip weighing 150 pounds at the rim would finish it weighing less than a pound at the edge of the hub. Under these conditions, experienced colonists would probably need only a single jump or two to get around the edge of the hub to the tube leading to the place where they want to go. Once in a "down" elevator, the process of weight change would run through in reverse. I imagine that taking this sort of elevator ride will turn out to be very popular with young people in the colony, and that riding the elevators will be as popular with them as riding around on subways is with children in cities today.

The clustering of dwellings will have many advantages besides easy travel. A village of two thousand is small enough so that most people will be able to know each other, leading to the kind of sense of community and closeness we associate with small towns. It would also give a natural structure for athletic rivalries that even those who live in big cities enjoy so much. I imagine the games between "Vail" and "Ventura" will be followed as avidly in the colony as the Green Bay Packer–Chicago Bear confrontations are on earth.

But the greatest advantage of clustering is that it will leave a good deal of the floor area of the colony open. Just how much depends on the details of the colony design, but it is not unreasonable to imagine that more than half of the four-mile periphery of the main ring will not contain dwellings. How the excess land will be used is largely a matter of speculation, of course. Some will surely be used to raise food and some will be used for recreation, but the actual mix between the two is impossible to predict. My own guess is that most of the food for the colony will actually be grown in small agricultural cylinders that are separate from the main ring, and that the prime land area in the main ring will be turned over to recreational uses of the colonists. The reason for this guess was already alluded to in the last chapter. The primary reason for building a colony will be to provide homes for a high-quality work force, and the homes will have to be attractive to bring in the kind of people who will be needed in space. The promise of a pleasant apartment surrounded by parks would go a long way toward fulfilling this goal. Consequently, the artist's conception of the colony as a place where clusters of dwellings are separated by open lands with trees and rivers may not be as farfetched as it might seem.

Let us do a little numerical exercise to see how this works. Suppose that there are ten thousand people in the colony and that we want to provide 500 square feet of dwelling space for each of them. This would be the type of floor space you might expect in a medium-sized suburban home in America today. The total floor space requirement, then, would be 5 million square feet. If the main ring of the colony were 180 feet high, then we could fit an eighteen-story building into it. This means that about 280,000 square feet of the main ring would have to be reserved for buildings. If the base of the ring is also 180 feet wide, then 1,555 feet—a little over a quarter mile—of the four-mile periphery would be occupied by houses. So the dwelling space need not be a huge apartment block. There is room to spread the buildings out and make them attractive while still leaving a substantial fraction of the main ring open.

The problem of providing pleasant housing in high-rise buildings with limited land area is one that architects have thought about for a long time—ever since human beings started living in cities. The problem can be stated quite simply: How do you put a lot of people together and still ensure that they have an acceptable level of privacy?

There have been many imaginative answers to this question. In southern European villages homes were built around courtyards, which gave the effect of shutting out the outside. Modern architects like Moshe Safdie, who designed the "Habitat" apartments as part of the Montreal World Fair in 1967, use the concept of the terraced apartment to achieve the same end. In this type of building every apartment has some open space in front of it—space that is actually the ceiling of the apartment below. In this way each homeowner can have his or her own little garden and view of the open lands of the colony. Apartments do not have to be dreary rectangular prisons, and in our space colony they surely will not be.

Construction

Although there will be enough room for space colonists to live in homes that are comfortable and even conventional by current standards, there will be important differences between homes in the colony and homes on earth. These differences will arise from a fact we have already discussed in some detail: the fact that the building materials in the colony will have to come from the moon.

We have already touched on some of the consequences of this fact. It means, for example, that wood cannot be used as a building material in the colony. Even if large trees are grown in the parks—and with 180 feet of headroom there is no reason why they should not be—it would take more than a century to accumulate enough wood to build a sizeable structure, even if parkland trees were to be cut.

It also means that plastics would not be used very much. Plastics are made from organic materials that do not exist on the moon, and the atoms that appear in them—primarily hydrogen and carbon—are much too valuable to be used for building. This, incidentally, at least partially answers one of the most frequent objections to the totally man-made environment of the space colony—that it would be too "plastic" to live in.

This does not mean that the buildings in the colony will have to be made from completely unfamiliar materials. We have already seen that the lunar materials are rich in the minerals needed to make all sorts of glass. Since the purpose of the houses will be primarily to provide privacy rather than to act as shelter—there will, after all, be no weather to speak of in the colony—we can expect that large glass windows and doors will be a feature of the colony apartments. NASA has already developed and used a cloth woven entirely from fiberglass, another substance that can be made easily from lunar materials. Called "beta cloth," it has the consistency of light canvas or heavy denim. It can be colored simply by including trace minerals in the melting pot when the fiberglass is made. Presumably, the large windows would be covered with drapes of beta cloth when privacy was desired. And by the time the colonies are built, there will surely be other materials like this available.

The actual weight-bearing parts of the apartment buildings—the walls and floors—will be made of precast slabs of material very much like concrete made from lunar quicklime and soil. In addition, there are enough clays in lunar soil to allow the fabrication of bricks. So with all of these materials, plus the aluminum and titanium that we have already talked about when we discussed the construction of the main ring, there should be no shortage of building materials for housing inside the colony.

The net result, then, is that homes in space will really not be all that different from homes on earth. There will be one-bedroom apartments for single people, one- and two-bedroom apartments for married couples, and larger dwellings for families with children. The materials from which the homes are built will be different, but this is nothing new. Humans have always built their homes out of the most easily obtainable materials in their environment, and in space metals and ceramics will take the place of wood and stone. The same will be true of furniture and other artifacts of daily life.

There will also be changes in the arts and crafts. Leather and woodworking will not be practiced in space on any widespread basis, but metal sculpture, pottery making, and glassworking either as a profession or as a hobby will be. The materials will change, but human creativity will stay the same.

A small river whose shores are lunar sand runs near the "equator" of this conceptual interior of a space settlement. Attractive living areas such as this will induce families to stay in space settlements for longer periods of time.

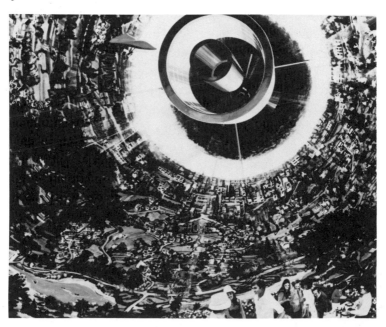

A Cautionary Thought

The discussion of the interior design of the satellite and individual dwellings we have just gone through has an important hidden assumption. It is the assumption that an effort will be made to make the space habitat as earthlike as possible. This is probably valid for the first colony built, since it will necessarily be populated by people who were born and reared on earth. They will be people like us, who would find life without grass and trees very wearing over long periods of time. We grew up in earthly surroundings and we would expect to have something not too radically different in any permanent home. In this sense, the first space colonists will be no different from the Europeans who immigrated to the United States and created their Little Italies, Little Polands, and Germantowns.

On the other hand, the descendants of those same immigrants for the most part now live in suburbs with no recognizable European influences. By the same token, we can expect that later generations of space dwellers may very well not need the same sort of open spaces that we require. They may, for example, find that working outside of the colony, in space, is all that is needed to repress feelings of claustrophobia while living in the colony. They may regard grass and trees as a sort of old-fashioned anachronism, akin to handlebar mustaches and high-button shoes. To them, the equivalent of a move to the suburbs may be quarters in a colony in which the entire interior space is filled with various private and public rooms, with shuttlecars or moving sidewalks to take people from one spot to another.

What this means is that we have to be a little skeptical of any claim that space colonies will always be the sort of roomy, parklike places we are describing here. The first one probably will be, and later ones may be. But in the final analysis, the move to space will be a new adventure for the human race and therefore very difficult to predict with any precision. After all, who would have been able to predict the existence of places like London or Manhattan at that time in the dim past when men first started moving from scattered farms and villages into cities?

7 | Eating High on the Hog

The question people most frequently ask when thinking about the idea of space colonies is: *Could the colony really be self-sufficient?* We know that recycling systems for air and water can be built; we have seen them in operation in manned satellites and submarines for many years. There is no reason in principle why similar systems could not operate indefinitely in a colony, with occasional replenishing of stocks from lunar materials. This means that questions about self-sufficiency really center around food, rather than around air and water. Food is definitely not recyclable in the sense that air and water are, and so it has to be grown or shipped in if the colonists are to survive.

If the colony could not grow the bulk of its own food, it would be pretty hopeless to think about living in space. The food requirements of a community of ten thousand people would come to roughly twenty-five tons per day—enough to fill a large truck. To ship this much material from earth would require sending up a heavy-lift launch vehicle every few weeks—a procedure that would be tremendously expensive and possibly entail a high level of damage to the earth's atmosphere. Besides, in a larger sense a colony that relied on shipments from earth for anything as essential as food would not be a colony in the way we are using the term. It would be an outpost more analagous to the scientific missions living at the South Pole, receiving all of their supplies by air, than to the first settlers in a new land.

So the colonists will most certainly have to grow their own food. The question then becomes how and where they will do so. We have seen that the main ring of the colony will have plenty of room for open spaces, and it could very well be that the first colony designs will call for intensive agricultural use of this space. In the long term, however, it is unlikely that the main ring will be used in this way. After all, it is the only place in the colony with earth-normal gravity and a slow rotation rate. It is, therefore, prime real estate. Using such space exclusively for farming would make about as much sense as plowing up Central Park in New York City and planting vegetables there. Consequently, in the long run we can expect that the colony's food supplies will come from areas outside of the main ring.

This does not mean, however, that there will be no agricultural work in the torus. Plants play important roles beyond that of supplying food. On the earth, their most important function in the ecosystem is to absorb carbon dioxide and give off oxygen. Consequently, they function as a natural recycling system for air. To a lesser extent, they play a role in the recycling of water as well, drawing it from the ground and allowing it to be evaporated into the air from their leaves. Given the large open area available in the main colony, it seems reasonable to expect that green plants will be used as an important part of the recycling systems. They have the enormous advantage of providing a system that is very close to fail-safe—the system will not shut down because of a blown fuse. They can also provide food and recreational areas at the same time that they are cleaning up the air.

In order to grow plants in the main ring, we will have to provide them with several essentials. Most important is the light necessary for the process of photosynthesis. The plants will also need water and various nutrients delivered to their roots and carbon dioxide to their leaves. The last requirement will, of course, be met automatically because the plants will be in contact with the carbon dioxide exhaled into the air by the colonists.

We have not yet discussed, however, how light will be delivered to the interior of the colony. There is, of course, an unlimited amount of sunlight in space, so the problem is simply one of getting the right amount into the main ring. The easiest design solution to this problem is to have large windows on the inside of the main ring—that is, on the "up" side of the ring as seen from the inside—and to have large nonrotating mirrors in space to reflect sunlight through them. The mirrors would be very lightweight structures, essentially reflecting plastic sheets stretched over a large open framework. They would be stationary in space and therefore would not have to be very strong. The window glass, of course, would be made from lunar materials. "Day" and "night" in the colony could then be regulated by moving shutters across the window spaces.

If large expanses of windows turn out to be undesirable— they might let in too much radiation—the same effect can be achieved by other means. For example, the nonrotating mirrors could be concave instead of flat, so that the sunlight is concentrated on small windows in the torus "ceiling." Once inside, another series of mirrors would diffuse the light again and spread it around the colony. In this way all of the necessary light could be brought in through a narrow slit of windows around the torus, greatly reducing the open area in the main ring framework. If even this was not enough, the concentrated sunlight could be run through a tunnel in the radiation shield of the type shown in figure 8. Such an arrangement could be used to bring in all the light the colony needed without letting cosmic rays in at all.

So the essentials of the growth process of light and carbon dioxide would be readily available in the main ring. This means that anything planted in dirt and watered could be made to grow there, since the conditions would be identical to those found on earth. The soil, of course, would originate on the moon, but plants have been grown in moon soil in laboratories on earth, so this should cause no problems.

As a matter of fact, plants can be grown in some rather surprising environments. Soil plays two essential roles in plant growth: it supports the plant physically, and it allows water and nutrients to reach the root system. But you do not

Figure 8

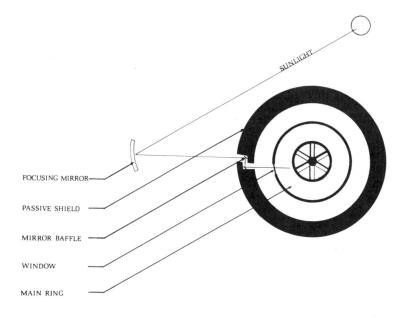

FOCUSING MIRROR

PASSIVE SHIELD

MIRROR BAFFLE

WINDOW

MAIN RING

have to have traditional black topsoil to do this. Plants can be grown in vermiculite, the kind of material used for kitty litter, or any loosely packed material that will allow water to flow through, carrying nutrients to the plants. Such systems of growing, called "hydroponics," have been known for a long time. They are used in the United States by a small but growing group of enthusiasts who lack the space for conventional gardens. It is also used extensively by many urban "back-to-the-land" groups who are trying to find ways to make urban dwellers more self-sufficient in the areas of food and energy. It is very likely that a high percentage of the colony's foodstuffs will be grown by this method.

So a possible agricultural system for the main ring might look something like this: part of the nonresidential area of the main ring is given over to hydroponic gardening. This would take place in tall, hangarlike buildings filled to the ceiling with racks of growing plants. The roots of the plants would be in a loosely packed material manufactured from lunar soils, and a continuous trickle of water would be run through the racks, carrying nutrients and moisture to the plants. The nutrients themselves would be the products of recycling the colony's waste materials, a process that would be familiar to any compost-minded gardener. Precisely controlled amounts of light would be brought into the building by mirrors, and the temperature and humidity would be controlled to provide optimum growing conditions for the plants. Every "afternoon" a series of ceiling pipes would provide a misty rain to keep the leaves moist. Given the ability to control growing conditions exactly, enterprises of this kind will surely be able to keep the colonists supplied with a continuous supply of fresh vegetables for their meals.

The other open spaces in the main ring could be used for agriculture as well, although, as we pointed out, they probably will not be. The parklands that we have described need not be totally unproductive as far as food is concerned, however. There are few environments on earth more pleasant than a well-kept orchard. Since the parklands will undoubtedly have trees in them, why not let those trees serve the double role of decoration and source of fruit? Given that the climate of the living area will be controlled, it is unlikely that trees that require a freeze in the winter, such as apples, will be able to grow. The fruit will more likely be the sort of thing we associate with the tropics—oranges, plums, olives, bananas, and so forth. Most of these trees have a relatively shallow root system and could grow quite easily in a few feet of dirt. Indeed, dwarf versions of these trees are often grown in tubs for decoration. So, fruit trees will definitely play a role in the life of the colony, providing a steady supply of fresh fruit to the colonists' menus.

In addition to these "official" activities, the colonists will undoubtedly use their terrace gardens individually to grow plants as well. The colony would be an ideal climate for tropical flowers and orchids, for example, and home vegetable gardens will probably be just as popular among the green thumb set in the colony as they are in any suburb. Some may try to raise space-consuming delicacies such as artichokes and asparagus—foods that may not be grown in the mass hydroponic tanks. Others may prefer to grow ornamental flowers for their decorative value. I would guess that gardening would be one of the main leisure activities among the colonists, just as it is on earth.

Given the large amount of flowering plants and trees that will be grown, it is likely that the colony will support a small apiary as well. In orchards on earth, beehives are kept just for the value that the bees have in the pollination process. Beehives, being relatively compact, can be maintained in almost any environment. They are frequently found in cities; I recall seeing a photograph of one kept by a hobbyist in the roof of a Manhattan apartment building. A well-managed hive can produce from fifty to eighty pounds of honey per year, more than enough to keep a family's sweet tooth satisfied. The partnership between man and honeybee, which began over five thousand years ago in Egypt, may well be carried into space.

The main part of the colonist's diet, grains and meat, could also be grown in the main ring if necessary. Rice has been used for centuries in Asia as a high-intensity source of grain. Since it supplies a high yield per acre, it would be ideal for the conditions in the colony, and will undoubtedly play a major role there.

The question of livestock will be discussed in more detail below, but those animals that can be raised by high-yield, high-intensity techniques will obviously be the favored source of meat. This means the colonists are likely to be raising pigs, chickens, and rabbits instead of cows. But as anyone who has ever lived downwind from a pigpen or chicken hatchery knows, there are some agricultural pursuits that can make life unpleasant for close neighbors. This fact, coupled with the high value of space in the main ring, leads to the suggestion that the great bulk of the colony's agricultural activity will take place in separate minicolonies devoted entirely to farming.

Since plants would not be affected by the Coriolis force, these agricultural structures would not be bound by the one-rotation-per-minute rule and could therefore be a good deal smaller than the main ring. Some typical designs call for structures in the shape of spheres or cylinders a few hundred yards across. A minicolony this size would have to rotate two or three times per minute to produce earth-normal gravity on its outer rim. This is too high a rotation rate for permanent occupancy, but it is not so high that people could not work inside.

The advantages of agricultural minicolonies are many. We have already pointed out that recreational and residential use of the main ring will have higher priority than agricultural. There are also some aesthetic disadvantages to having some agricultural operations there. But more importantly, having agricultural operations located in several small structures away from the main colonies means that several radically different environments can be provided for agriculture. For example, it may turn out that plant growth rates can be increased significantly by lowering the level of pseudogravity

A colony's food supply will not depend on shipments from earth. Instead, the colonists will probably grow their own food in agricultural minicolonies. Shuttles will be used for other important missions, including placing satellites in orbit, as illustrated below.

to 80 or 90 percent of earth-normal. This would be impossible to do in the main ring, of course, but quite easy to do in a small separate agricultural cylinder. By the same token, it could well be that animals raised in conditions of higher-than-normal gravity would develop more muscle than those raised at earth-normal. A separate ''ranch'' cylinder could then provide this environment for them.

But the most important advantage to the agricultural cylinder concept is the fact that it provides many isolated food-growing operations. To use an appropriate metaphor, the colonists would not be putting all of their eggs into one basket. If a problem arose in one cylinder, it would be contained and would not necessarily damage the others. For example, if a particular disease destroyed the crop in the wheat-growing cylinder, the cylinder could simply be opened up to the vacuum and cold of space. This would effectively sterilize the cylinder so that the next crop would not encounter similar difficulties, but it would not affect food being raised elsewhere. This sort of protection is particularly important in closed ecological systems like space colonies because of the operation of something engineers call ''Murphy's Law.'' The law says that if something can go wrong in any situation, it will. So despite all precautions taken, sooner or later some sort of contamination will reach the colony. Perhaps some diseased seed will slip through the inspection, or the eggs of some pest like the vine borer will come through. It is extremely important that the colony be designed so that containment and elimination of such problems can be carried out easily.

How much total space—main ring plus agricultural cylinders—would the colonists have to devote to growing their own food?

On earth, the best farmlands are located in the rich black

topsoil of the midwestern corn belt. In a good year, a farmer in Iowa or Illinois can harvest 140 bushels of corn for each acre of land—about 3.5 tons. This amounts to about twenty pounds of corn per day, averaged over the entire year. But farmers in space will have some advantages that their midwestern counterparts can only dream of. For example, they will have a continuous growing season, so that their land will not have to lie idle six months of the year. For another, they will have total control of the weather on their farms. They will be able to have rain when rain is needed and sunshine when it is not. They will be able to control the length of night and day as their crops mature. In other words, the space farmers will be able to grow their crops under conditions like those found in laboratories on earth.

And yields under laboratory conditions can be astonishing. Some as high as several thousand pounds per acre *per day* have been reported by plant scientists in the United States. This is to be compared with the 20 pounds per day in the midwest and the 125 pounds per day produced under the best field conditions in experimental plots outside of the laboratory.

With production at only 125 pounds per acre per day it would require about four hundred acres to feed the colony. But if we assume that the colonists will be able to reproduce the best laboratory conditions that will have been obtained on earth, this requirement drops to a mere fifty acres—about one-eighth of the area of the main ring. From this exercise, we see that agriculture on the colony will not be a scramble to provide subsistance meals made from algae and yeast mold. The colonists' diets will include most of the fruit, vegetables, and grains that we are used to. There will be plenty of wheat flour for baked goods, and crops of sugar beets will be raised to prevent the colony's children from being deprived of sweets. In fact, the only difference you would notice between your diet today and what you would have on the colony would be in the type of meat that was served.

There is a vast amount of land in the United States that is too dry to be used for anything but grazing. Stretching northward from Texas to Montana, the high plains sustain herds of cattle, and beef has become the principal meat in the American diet. It is important to realize, however, that the prevalence of steaks and hamburgers in our experience is due to a geographical accident. The fact is that the high plains simply can not be used to raise any other kind of food, so if it takes forty acres of range to produce one steer, then the forty acres will be used for that purpose. There just is not any alternative—it is cattle or nothing.

But in Europe and Asia, where large areas of unusable land do not exist, beef plays a much smaller role in the diet. When you start to compare animals in terms of pounds of protein per pound of feed, you find that there are many animals that are more efficient producers of protein than beef cattle. Probably the most efficient animal from this point of view is the rabbit. A rabbit hutch three feet on a side can easily hold a doe and her litter. Given the legendary speed with which rabbits multiply, it should come as no surprise that under these conditions, feeding the rabbits alfalfa, meat can be produced at the rate of 150 pounds per acre per day. And although caring for caged rabbits does not have the same panache as riding the open range, rabbits raised in this way could provide a pound of meat a day for each colonist on a little over sixty acres of land.

Goats, pigs, and chickens are other animals that can be raised efficiently in confined spaces. Goats have the advantage of producing milk as well as meat, while chickens supply eggs. Thus it is possible for the colonists to have a range of familiar dairy products like butter and cheese. An entirely new type of cheese might even be made under conditions of weightlessness, in which case we could have the paradoxical situation of the space colony exporting a gourmet food product back to earth.

So, as far as protein goes, the colonists' diet will probably be more like that found in Middle Eastern countries than in the United States. It will be heavy in mutton and pork, but light in beef. In fact, this is probably the only difference in eating habits you would notice if you were to be taken to the colony today.

I do not think it is impossible that some cows will eventually be taken to the colony. For one thing, dairy cattle are much more prolific producers of milk than goats. For another, we have seen that the first colony is likely to be designed with the comfort and tastes of the residents very much in mind. The first people aboard will have been raised on beef-rich diets, and will probably want to continue enjoying an occasional steak. Consequently, it is likely that a few cattle will be raised in feedlots for luxury dining, and that a colonist will celebrate a special occasion with a steak dinner the way a modern American might celebrate with pheasant under glass.

There is another way that cows could be useful in the colony. If there are really going to be a hundred-plus acres of parkland and orchards, somebody or something is going to have to cut all that grass. Keeping a small herd of cows and sheep to take care of this job would kill two birds with one stone: it would eliminate the need for lawnmowers, and it would provide a little more meat for the larder.

8 | The Energy Crisis (or Lack of It) in Space

One of the points to which we have come back over and over again in our discussion has been the abundance of energy in space. This has figured prominently in our descriptions of space factories, of building operations, and in our preferred scenario for the events leading to the building of the colony itself. Since the entire effort will stand or fall on the availability of energy, it is probably worthwhile for us to look at how the sunlight in space might be tapped.

In 1968, Dr. Peter Glaser of the Arthur D. Little Corporation first proposed what has come to be known as the solar power satellite system, or SPSS for short. He began by pointing out that there are many problems with the development of solar power on earth. The most important of these is that any solar receiving system must be inoperative at night and during cloudy weather. Consequently, extensive and costly systems have to be built to store energy collected while the sun is shining so that the energy can be used when the sun is not shining. In space, on the other hand, there is no night and day, nor is there weather of any sort. The full power of the sun's rays can be extracted around the clock, which gives space-based solar energy systems an important advantage over their ground-based counterparts.

The SPSS was not proposed with space colonies in mind, of course, but it has two important features that bear on our discussion. First, a large-scale SPSS designed to supply power to earth would necessarily entail large numbers of people working in space—a necessary prerequisite to the building of a colony. Secondly, when the SPSS is perfected, the colony will have a source for the energy it needs. An added bonus would be that a single satellite would provide enough power to run the lunar mining operation, mass driver included. Consequently, the SPSS is really an integral part of the space colony idea, and it is well worth our while to understand how it works.

Solar Cells

How does something as ordinary as sunlight get converted to electricity, anyway? The basic tool for accomplishing this, either on earth or in space, is the solar cell. Stripped of everything but essentials, a solar cell is made from two thin layers of material, usually but not always silicon, which has been prepared in a special way. The net effect of this arrangement is that sunlight falling on the cell shakes electrons loose in the material, and these electrons then move off into an outside circuit, where they are detected as an electrical current. The details of how the cell works are interesting, too. In essence, things are arranged so that most of the work involved in generating the electricity is done by forces associated with the atoms themselves, with no energy input other than sunlight.

Let us take a silicon cell as being typical of all solar cells. Silicon is an atom that has four free electrons in the outermost orbit. When silicon atoms come together, their electrons interact in such a way as to bind the atoms together into a hard material not too different from diamond, which is made from carbon atoms. One way to picture the binding process is to think of two neighboring atoms as exchanging one electron each with each other. This process generates what chemists call a "covalent bond" between the neighbors. In the figures to follow we will represent a covalent bond as a double line between neighboring atoms—the two lines to remind us that two electrons are involved, one from each atom.

A silicon crystal would look something like the diagram in figure 9, then. The atoms would be evenly spaced and the four electrons in each atom would be shared with the four neighboring atoms. All the electrons in the material would go into forming the bonds, and none would be free to move about.

Now if light from the sun strikes the crystal as shown, it may knock one of the electrons loose. The result of such a collision is that now an electron is free to move around the crystal, but at the same time one of the electrons is missing from a covalent bond. If light streams into a simple block of silicon as shown above, the electrons created will wander around until they encounter a broken bond, at which point they will fall back in. An equilibrium is thus reached, but

Figure 9

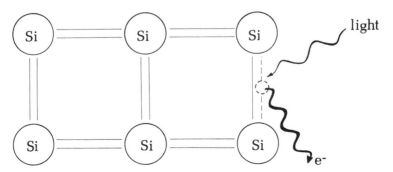

there is no current generated. Every electron eventually joins up with a silicon atom somewhere.

In order to get a piece of silicon like this to generate an electric current, we have to make some special preparations. Two batches of molten silicon are prepared. In one batch a small amount of a material like phosphorous, which has five electrons in its outer orbit, is added, while in another a small amount of aluminum, which has three electrons in its outer orbit, goes in. When thin layers of silicon made from these two materials are joined together, we get something like the situation shown in figure 10. On one side of the junction an occasional silicon atom is replaced by phosphorous, and the extra electron from the phosphorous atom, which is not nec-

Figure 10

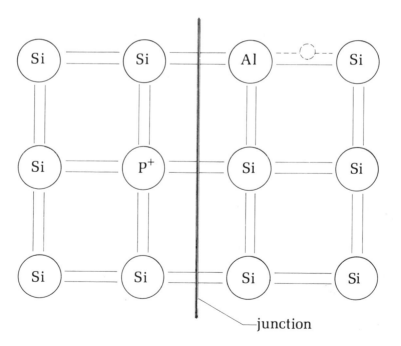

junction

essary for the binding process, just goes wandering off. On the other side the aluminum atoms lack one electron, so there is a vacancy wherever one of them replaces the silicon. Eventually the electrons from the phosphorus near the junction wander over and fill these vacancies and we are left with a junction in which positive phosphorus atoms (positive because they have lost one electron) sit on one side and negative aluminum atoms (negative because they have gained an electron) sit on the other. A device built in this manner is called a junction diode.

Now if an electron is shaken loose by sunlight on the left-hand side, it is pulled toward the right by the positive phosphorus atoms, building up enough speed to be pushed through the junction. If it starts on the right, it is repelled by the negative aluminum atoms. The net effect of the junction, then, is to take any electrons created in the material and move them to the right. If we attached wires to the silicon as shown in figure 11, we could then get an electrical current. In essence, this is a solar cell. Cells built according to the principles we have outlined here have already enjoyed widespread use in satellites and are undergoing intensive development for mass production on earth. The essential feature is that once the cell is made, all the energy is supplied by sunlight and all the forces are supplied by the arrangement of the atoms. No outside intervention is necessary.

So getting energy from the sun would seem to be pretty easy. You just make enough solar cells to collect the amount of energy you need, put them in the light, and sit back and watch the electrons flow. But like so many other things that are simple in principle, there are some flies in the ointment when it comes to building the real thing.

One problem is that, even in space, sunlight is a pretty diffuse form of energy. For example, even if we could con-

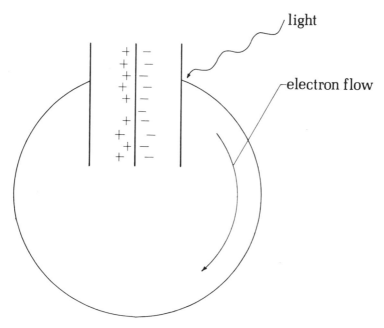

Figure 11

vert sunlight to electricity at 100 percent efficiency, it would take a sheet of silicon about three feet on a side to power an ordinary toaster. This is why designers of solar power satellites are driven to talk about very large structures.

But that is not the end of the story. Solar cells, no matter how well made, can never convert all of the sunlight that falls on them to electricity. The reasons for this have nothing to do with engineering skill, but depend on the basic laws of physics. For example, it turns out that about one-third of the sunlight falling on a cell comes in forms whose energy is not great enough to cause an electron to break away from its parent silicon atom. This means that one-third of the sunlight hitting the cell will never get converted into electrical energy, but will just heat the cell. From this factor alone we can see that the maximum efficiency of a solar cell must be below 67 percent. Other effects serve to bring this figure even lower. For example, once an electron has been shaken loose and starts its journey through the cell, there is always a chance that it will encounter the vacancy left behind by another electron and fall into it, recombining with a silicon atom to reform a bond. By the time all of the effects that lower the efficiency of a solar cell are taken into account, we find that the theoretical best efficiency of a typical solar cell must be roughly 20 to 25 percent. In other words, between four-fifths and three-fourths of all the sunlight that falls on the cell is wasted as far as the production of electricity is concerned. So if we want to generate a certain amount of electricity, we have to have a collector four to five times as big as we might think we need in order to overcome the inefficiencies of even the best possible cell. To use the example given above, if we wanted to power a toaster with such a cell we would need a sheet of silicon over six feet on a side to do it.

A real solar cell, made by real people, will not measure up to the theoretical ideal. In addition, if that solar cell has to be mass-produced—a requirement guaranteed by the dilute nature of solar energy—then it may fall well below the ideal. Within the next few years it is likely that solar cells whose efficiency is about 10 percent will be produced, by processes similar to those used in making photographic film, in rolls a hundred feet long and eight feet wide. It is this sort of material that will be used in the space colony power systems. For reference, a 10 percent solar cell, in order to power a toaster, would have to be about ten feet on a side—about as big as a small room.

SPSS

It seems, then, that if we are going to make use of the abundant energy in space, we are going to have to build a very large collector. To see how such a system might work, let us take a look at the so-called "reference system" for the SPSS. This is the system that engineers use in dealing with questions about solar power satellites, and it may or may not be similar to the one that will be built eventually.

The reference system is designed to deliver five thousand megawatts of electrical power, which is as much as five large nuclear reactors or coal-burning plants. The original plans call for a system of about thirty thousand tons. An open platform will support silicon solar cells in a "venetian blind" configuration. In order to get the five thousand megawatts on the ground, the actual size of the collector will be huge— roughly six miles by two miles. This gives a platform area of

Solar power satellite systems such as this will be used to collect light energy from the sun and convert it to electricity that can be used on earth. When the SPSS is perfected, it will be able to supply colonies with the energy they need.

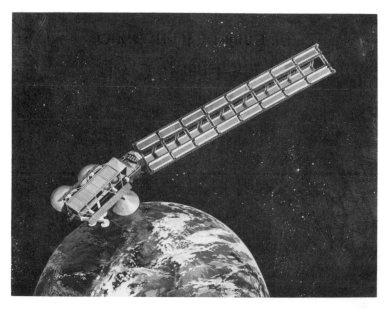

20.8 square miles (about the size of a small town), of which 20.4 square miles will be covered with silicon—over seven thousand tons worth. The electrical current will be fed to two antennae, each over a half mile across, where it will be converted to microwaves. These will then be beamed to earth.

The transmission of power by microwaves is not a particularly difficult technology. The receiving station on earth would have to be about six miles across, but the receivers themselves are very simply pieces of wire that could be manufactured by the billions in any advanced nation today. In fact, Peter Glaser is fond of recalling the time a Japanese industrialist heard his talk on SPSS and asked how many receivers would be needed. On learning that it would take millions of them to make a single receiving area, his next question was, "When do you want delivery?"

So the solar power satellite is something that engineers agree could be built, probably by the year 2000. It follows, then, that when space colonies are built they will use modifications of the SPSS for their own energy needs. Of course, five thousand megawatts is much more energy than a community of ten thousand people would need, so the power satellites used in the colonies would be smaller than the reference satellite system we have been describing. In addition, there would be no need to convert the output of the solar cells into microwaves and then back into electricity—a process that loses about 20 percent of the original energy. The power source for the colony would probably feed directly into the electrical grid in the torus.

In fact, the only difference you would notice in the electrical system is that it would run on DC, the sort that comes from batteries, rather than the more familiar AC used in American households. The shape of the plugs and sockets would be a little different, and perhaps the motors in appliances would not be the same, but other than that the home-owners in the colony would regard their power utility system in much the same way as their earthbound counterparts: It is never noticed or thought about unless the bulb does not go on when you throw the switch.

Finally, we note that the SPSS gives us a clue as to what the main economic activity of the first colonists might be. They would be in the business of exporting electrical power back to earth—power that can be had for the asking in space, but which is needed here on the ground.

9 | All Work and No Play Makes Jack a Dull Boy

The workaday world on the colony will really not be so different from the one we already know about on earth. Many of the colonists will have familiar jobs—raising food, providing medical care, teaching, and keeping records. Others will work in the space factories, manufacturing power satellites and communications equipment to pay the colony's way by selling the products of space to an energy-hungry earth. Perhaps some people will be involved in mining asteroids—an activity we will talk about in more detail later. But all of these forms of work, from tending the computers that keep track of the colony's payroll to prospecting among the asteroids, will have one thing in common: No one will work all the time, and consequently everyone will need to have some sort of arrangements for spending his or her leisure time.

It is one of the amusing facts about the space colony idea that more creative thinking has gone into the question of recreation in the habitat than to any other single issue. Consequently, there is a wealth of ideas about the way that the unique features of the space environment will be used when the colonists quit working and set out to have some fun.

Intellectual Activities

The colonists will, by and large, be people who have high levels of education. This means that the leisure-time activities that we usually associate with intellectuals—music, theater, reading—will be in great demand in the colony. On the other hand, simple physical isolation will ensure that this leisure activity takes somewhat different forms from those we are used to.

Take reading as an example. Those of us who enjoy spending some of our spare time with a book are used to visiting a bookstore or a library to "stock up." But a traditional book is a pretty bulky thing. It is unlikely that it would be considered economical to haul an entire library up from earth. Besides, paper is made from wood pulp—a substance that will have to be used very sparingly in space.

Does this mean that the colonists will have to give up reading for recreation? Not at all. It just means that they will not do it in the traditional way. The public library on the colony will not be a book-lined room, but the memory banks of a large computer. A colonist who wants to curl up with a good book will just sit down at his personal computer output and ask for a display of titles. He will then pick the one he wants to read and instruct the computer to display it on the output tube. It is even possible that he will be able to instruct the computer to print a copy of the book to read—a copy that will be returned for recycling once he is done with it. A system like this would not require anything more than a radio link between earth and the library computer. No bulky books would have to be lifted into orbit, but the readers in the colony would still have access to the latest bestsellers, since a computer memory can be updated continuously. They would probably even be able to read all of the new fiction set in the exotic surroundings of a space colony, although they might see such writings more in the line of humor than of serious drama.

The library could also be expected to hold the latest magazines from earth, as well as the daily papers. There would be no need, therefore, for the colonists to be out of touch with the home planet at all.

The concept of an electronic link between the colony and the earth is crucial for other types of entertainment besides reading. The idea that entertainment should be electronic rather than live is not a difficult one to grasp in the age of television. But would the colony be too far away to receive television broadcasts from earth? The answer to this question is no. Although the distance from earth to the colony will be greater than that to any receiver on earth, the colony will always be in the line of sight of some earth-based transmitter. This means that as soon as the signal has gone through a few miles of atmosphere, it will have clear sailing into deep space. In addition, even a very weak signal can be picked up in space, provided that the receiving antenna is large enough. Since building large antennae is something that we expect the colonists to be very good at, it is very likely that television reception in space will be better than it is in some rural locations in the United States.

Of course, the fact that the dwellings will be inside of a solid metal torus does mean that individual television sets will not be able to pick up signals. It is more likely that a single large antenna will serve the entire colony, with the distribution of signals to individual dwellings being accomplished by a cable system not unlike the ones already in use in many American cities.

The net result of all of this would be an electronic web uniting the colony with the mainstream of culture on earth. The colonists would see live broadcasts of the best orches-

*One kind of work the first space colonists will engage in is the
building of solar power satellite systems. This artist's concept depicts the
arrival of cargo from low earth orbit to the SPS fabrication facility in
geosynchronous orbit.*

tras, the latest singing sensations, and first-run movies. They
would be as much a part of earth's culture as are people living in small towns in America today. There would be no
"culture shock" when colonists made visits back "home."

There is no question, then, that the colonists will have as
much cultural contact with earth as they want. When it comes
to personal visits, however, the situation will be different.
There is no chance that someone will put the Chicago Sym-
phony aboard a rocket for a concert in the colony—the cost
would be prohibitive. Even visits by solitary musicians or
actors would be out of the question. So for live performances, the colonists will have to fall back on their own
resources. The only analogue to this situation might be the
behavior of the European diplomatic corps in isolated capitals
of the world during the last century. They, too, were physi-

cally isolated from their homelands. The accounts of diplomatic life in Kabul or Dar es Salaam abound with descriptions of amateur theatricals, play readings, and chamber music supplied by people from the various embassies. I expect that it will be the same way in the space colony. In a population of ten thousand there are bound to be many people with musical and theatrical talent, so it is safe to say that the electronic "culture" in the colony will be supplemented by live performances by the colonists themselves. Eventually, we might even expect that plays, books, music, and other types of things we normally associate with the cultural life would be produced in the colony.

Athletics

A sound mind in a sound body. Since the time of the Greeks this has been held up as a goal for which human beings should strive. The jogging and physical fitness craze in the United States right now is just one manifestation of the human need for and interest in physical exercise. There is no reason to expect that space colonists will be any different in this regard.

The space environment will provide ample opportunities for physical activities. Some of these will be familiar and some will be new. From what we know about the colony design, we can make some intelligent guesses about what the colonists will do to keep in shape.

The first thing we can say is that sports that require a great deal of open space will simply not be available in space. There will be no hiking, backpacking, or mountain climbing in the torus. Another popular sport, hunting, will certainly not be pursued by the colonists. For one thing, there will be no wild animals. For another, there will be no location in the colony out of rifle range of human dwellings, so safety considerations alone lead us to this conclusion. Finally, the chance of a stray shot puncturing the colony wall would be too great to allow unrestrained shooting. I would not be surprised if firearms were banned in space for this reason alone.

But having excluded these sports, there are so many others left to choose from that the colonists won't miss them at all. Take jogging as an example. The colony will be an ideal place for this sport. Stepping out from your front door, you would begin by choosing the direction, clockwise or counterclockwise, in which you wanted to go. On your run you would encounter no automobiles. The colony weather would always be fair, with a temperature at seventy degrees—ideal running conditions. You would have a choice of terminating your run at any of the elevator hubs, which would be spaced about three-quarters of a mile apart, or going the full four miles around the rim, in which case you would be back at your apartment. There will probably be a "Four-Mile Club" for runners, as well as an annual "Around the Rim" footrace.

By the same token, there will be plenty of open space in the colony for a track, so that the traditional track and field sports could be pursued. The effects of the Coriolis force (see Chapter 2) will be so small that even the best discus or javelin throw would be indistinguishable from its counterpart on earth. A long list of team sports—football, soccer, basketball, hockey—could be played in the colony if there was a demand for them. The 180-foot-high "ceiling" in the torus would allow as much headroom for high fly balls and punts as do many of the indoor arenas in which these sports are now played.

In fact, the only complicating factor for conventional athletics in the colony would come in those sports that involve high-speed projectiles. We have already discussed the fact that the Coriolis force would put an additional curve on a fast pitch in baseball. By the same token, tennis, handball, and squash would have an additional but rather small complication from the same effect. A Wimbledon champion coming to the colony to play would have to adjust his game if he expected to keep on winning.

But by far the most interesting aspects of sports in the colonies will be those that are unique to the space environment. In particular, the availability of large spaces whose gravity is different from that on earth opens up all sorts of interesting possibilities for new kinds of athletic competitions. For example, in the very center of the colony hub will be a large enclosed space that has a normal atmosphere but zero gravity. There will undoubtedly be some pretty fierce competition for the use of this part of the colony. Scientists will want it for experiments, industrialists for manufacturing, and the average colonists for recreation. Since other zero-gravity space can be provided in a nonrotating minicolony that is separate from the main ring, there is a pretty good chance that the recreational use will win out. So, what kinds of sports could be played in zero gravity?

Gerard O'Neill suggests that this central zero-g room could be devoted to a swimming pool. It would certainly be a strange kind of pool. There would be enough pseudogravity around the edge of the pool to hold the water down, more or less, but if you were swimming along and looked "up," you would see your friends swimming on the "ceiling." Because you would weigh less than a pound, you could probably boost yourself out of the water with your arms, fly across the pool, and land in the water on the other side. One of the favorite games would be to get going just fast enough so that air resistance would bring you to a stop right at the midpoint of the pool, where there is exactly zero gravity and where every direction is "down." There might even be an interesting variation of "king-of-the-hill," where swimmers would try to stay at the center as long as possible, evading attempts by their friends to bring them down. The lifeguards in a pool like this would have their hands full!

The zero-g swimming pool is certainly an interesting concept, but given the scarcity of water in the colony it is not obvious that it would be built—at least not in the first-generation structure. Another possible use for a zero-g sports arena would be as an arena for space polo, which would be a cross between three-dimensional basketball and water polo. Players could shove off from the sides of the spherical arena, timing their pushes to keep themselves in the playing area for

Space polo court

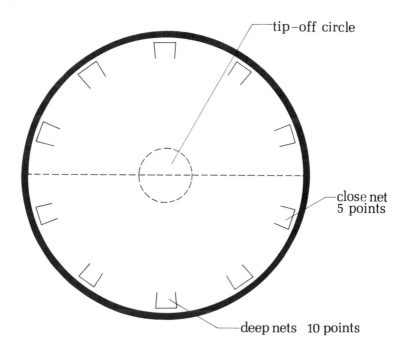

tip–off circle

close net
5 points

deep nets   10 points

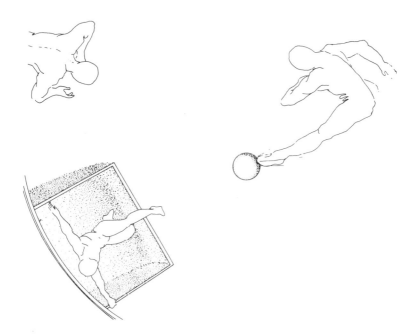

Space polo will be a sport unique to the space colony environment. Matches between teams of different villages in a colony or even between teams of different colonies may lead to a sports event as popular as the World Series or Super Bowl are on earth.

a maximum amount of time. The object of each team would be to put the ball into any one of a number of goals on the opponents' side of the sphere. The farther into the opponents' territory the goal is, the more points are awarded, so there would be room for strategy in the game . . . do you put your effort into making the big play for a deep goal, or pick off easy points in goals near midfield? Similarly, by having fewer goaltenders than goals, the defensive team has to decide whether to guard the deep, high-point nets or the close, easily hit but low-point ones. Given the speed with which the players could change positions in the three-dimensional playing field, space polo would be a very fast-moving, exciting game to watch. It would also require a fair amount of skill and experience in zero-gravity conditions, so it would truly be a game of space. You can amuse yourself by thinking up other types of games that could be played in the free-fall conditions of the colony's hub. What would zero-g, three-dimensional frisbee look like?

One aspect of sports in the colony that has not been explored in any detail is the possibility of having living space available where the gravity is greater than earth-normal. We mentioned the possibility, for example, that raising animals under these conditions might be more efficient than it would be under normal gravity. This opens the interesting possibility of having athletes train in heavy gravity, which we can call "super-g" conditions. Weight training—that is, the development of muscular strength by use of weight-lifting techniques—is already a recognized part of athletic preparation in almost any sport. Imagine the advantage a gymnast who was used to being fifty pounds heavier than his normal weight would have in competitions with those raised on earth. Colony athletes would probably start bringing home quite a few gold medals from future Olympic competitions—provided, of course, that they were allowed to participate. Students from the colony would probably have an easy time winning athletic scholarships at earthside universities, and you might even have a situation where serious athletes from earth would spend time in the colony just to make use of the super-g training facilities. One of the side effects of the development of space could be the hundred-foot shot put and the twenty-foot pole vault.

We began this discussion by pointing out that many traditional outdoor activities like hunting and backpacking will not be available in the colony. This is true, but it takes a rather narrow view of what constitutes the "outdoors." For the colonists, the entire sweep of deep space is the "outdoors," and I would be very surprised if recreational activities centered on the outside of the colony did not become quite popular. Space camping, for example, might be a lot of fun. Using small, low-powered vehicles that would double as basic transportation to the space factories during the week, entire families might take off for a weekend in free fall, getting away from the crush of the colony and into "God's Country" in space. Amateur astronomy would probably be a popular pastime on such excursions, and the lack of an obscuring atmosphere would make it even more rewarding than it is on earth. Moving about in space may take the place of swimming as a leisure-time activity, and we can expect that ingenious colonists will devise many other things to do in this unique environment. After all, people who were able to conceive of the snowmobile are not going to lose their creativity when they leave the surface of the earth. Whatever happens, the innate need of the human race to devise new and interesting ways to play virtually guarantees an entire new field of leisure activity in space.

10 | A Day in the Life of the Taylors

The colony has been in existence for twenty years. William and Elizabeth Taylor were one of the first couples to live in it, and their son Tom was one of the first children to be born in space. Let us follow a typical day to see what life on the colony would be like.

William Taylor, engineer
Bill Taylor rolls over and looks at the electric clock next to the bed. It reads seven o'clock Greenwich Mean Time—the universal time standard used in space. The large mirrors outside of the torus have already begun swinging into their "daytime" position, bringing light into the colony in the spaceside version of dawn. He can see the steadily brightening light through the beta cloth curtains covering the large glass patio doors that make up one wall of the bedroom. Leaving his wife asleep, he goes into the bathroom in the center of their three-bedroom apartment.

First he shaves with an electric razor—there is plenty of electricity in the colony. Next he takes a shower, but because water has to be used carefully, he does it navy style: first a quick rinse to get himself wet, then no water while he applies the soap, and then another quick rinse to get the soap off. He

96

pulls on a pair of the standard blue beta cloth coveralls that the colonists prefer for everyday wear. Since it is Elizabeth's turn to make breakfast, he goes out onto the patio space in front of the apartment. The light is now up to full daytime level, and he can see the sweep of the colony as it curves out of view in the distance. He pauses to admire the scene.

Beneath his patio, the apartment complex of Ventura falls away in a series of terraces. Six stories and sixty feet below, the building ends and the parkland begins. Looking down, only the tops of the trees are visible, but he knows that beneath them there are walking paths and open spaces. Farther away he sees the large agricultural building where Elizabeth works and then the towers of Vail, the neighboring village.

He sets to work on his garden. The even temperature in the colony makes year-round vegetable gardening possible, and the artichokes look like they will be ready to serve to the company this weekend. Stooping, he pulls out a few weeds that, in spite of all the precautions taken to keep the colony uncontaminated, have managed to get in and spread themselves around. As a gardener, he is sometimes amused by the idea that the end result of the human move into space may be to spread crabgrass around the solar system.

The sounds from inside tell him that the rest of the family is up. He goes into the kitchen and helps bring the breakfast out to the table set on the patio. There is, of course, no reason not to leave furniture outside, since it "rains" on the apartments only infrequently and with much advance notice, and even then only briefly, to clean things off. The breakfast consists of fresh orange juice from the colony orchards, toast with honey from the apiary, oatmeal, and milk from the colony goatherd. The dishes are ceramic, of course, made from lunar materials by a colony craftsman. The Taylors much prefer the handmade items to the mass-produced dishes. In the colony both materials and energy are cheap. Only human labor is expensive, which explains why handmade goods are so highly valued.

Leaving his apartment, he walks down the interior corridor of the building to the elevator, descending to a basement level. He steps onto a moving sidewalk, which carries him to the large room where the main hub elevators stop. After a short wait he enters one of the large elevators, scarcely noting the padding on the walls, floor, and ceiling—padding designed to protect the careless rider from the effects of changes in gravity. The doors close and the journey begins. At the start, the motors have to pull the elevator at full weight, so they move relatively slowly. As the trip progresses, the passengers feel themselves getting lighter and lighter, but the elevator moves faster and no one floats off of the floor. The half-mile journey takes a few minutes and by the time it ends everyone is, for all practical purposes, in free-fall weightlessness. For Bill Taylor this is no new experience. He will remain weightless for the rest of his working day in space. For other passengers it is just a temporary phase to go through on the way back down to their workplace on the main ring. But whether they work inside the ring or in space, all of the passengers are so used to the weightless condition that as soon as the elevator doors open they all push off down the appropriate corridors with the long, effortless glides that mark the free-fall veteran.

Bill takes a corridor that leads him to the space access port at the "bottom" of the hub. Here he gets into his working clothes—a spacesuit of light flexible material that resembles the bulky suits worn by the first astronauts about as much as modern pilots' garb resembles the leather jackets and scarves worn by their predecessors in the First World War. A helmet with "Taylor–Project Engineer" stenciled on it goes under his arm as he joins a group of his coworkers waiting for the factory shuttle to come to dock.

They can see it approaching through the window: a large spherical ship propelled by old-fashioned chemical rockets. Like much of the equipment designed to house and transport people in space, it provides protection from cosmic radiation by using a magnetic field set up by powerful but small superconducting magnets. The magnetic field is not visible, of course, but knowing it is there is important to people like Bill Taylor. Like anyone else who works around radiation, he carries an exposure meter in his suit. The meter is checked periodically by health workers, and if he has managed to accumulate too high a dose, he has to be rotated to a desk job inside the ring for a while. To an "outdoorsman" like Bill, that is a fate to be avoided at all costs, so he is always careful about radiation.

As the shuttle approaches, an access tube snakes out from the hub and attaches to the entrance port. As per regulations, the travelers seal their helmets so that they can breath in case of sudden loss of pressure and glide in. The "seats" in the shuttle are just straps to hold people in place during the mild accelerations that the craft undergoes, because if you do not weigh anything there is no need to sit down to take a load off of your feet, is there?

With a barely perceptible lurch, the shuttle begins its trip. A short period of acceleration brings it to its cruising speed of about sixty miles per hour. The rockets cut off, again with a barely perceptible lurch, and the passengers relax for the ten-minute coast to the space factory site. The colony fades in the rear, and by the time they reach the main factory terminal ten miles away it looks no bigger than the size of your fist held at arm's length. The space manufacturing terminal is just a large hollow sphere where the shuttle can dock and unload its passengers, who then scatter to the various work locations in smaller "space cabs."

In fact, approaching the space manufacturing center would be a very confusing process for a visitor to the colony. From a distance it resembles nothing so much as a collection of tin cans, mirrors, and loose pieces of metal strewn in space. Yet when the ship comes closer, each of these pieces of floating debris is seen to be huge—each a factory in and of itself. For example, in one large nonrotating cylinder the weightless environment is used to fabricate pharmaceuticals and materials that simply cannot be made to combine on earth. These new materials are already crucial in the development of entire new industries. The mirrors are seen to be capable of concentrating enough sunlight to melt the ores brought in from the moon, the start of a metallurgical process that eventually produces the finished metals and other materials needed to keep the factories going. Already some of this material is being stockpiled for the construction of another colony—a move that will double the population of space dwellers. Off to the right, Bill can see the webbed structure of a solar power satellite under construction—the project for which he is now responsible. When it is finished, it will be towed into orbit around the moon, where it will power a mass driver now nearing completion. As his small vehicle approaches the main computer center for the project, the full scale of the vast platform becomes apparent. The racks of aluminum girders and silicon sheets seem to stretch into the far distance.

The control center for the project, like so many of the buildings in the factory area, does not rotate, so people working there must be adaptable to the weightless environment. It is surrounded with a passive radiation shield like the main colony ring, and its occupants can see what is happening outside through the use of television monitor cameras. When

Bill comes in the crew is already starting up the remote control robots, which do most of the mundane assembly work in space. This week's operation is pretty routine: all that has to be done is to install a new section of platform so that it will be ready to receive the solar panels now being assembled in another part of the factory complex. The new girders are floating in space six miles from the control center, next to the new section of the satellite. They were left there by the space tug that hauled them over from the nearby girder fabrication facility where they had been made, inspected, and tested. They were left in space in much the same way as a load of bricks would be left on the ground at a modern earthside construction site, waiting in a pile until they are needed. After all, something left in space will just float in place—there is nowhere for it to fall.

The control center is a series of panels next to television monitors. Each panel controls one of the large construction robots out on the platform, and each is manned by a member of the construction crew. A sign over the door reads *Helmets must be worn at all times in this building,* but no one pays much attention to it. Bill takes his helmet off as he comes in and goes to the main computer console to go through the morning status report on the project. Half an hour later he is just going over some of the performance tests on a recently completed bank of solar cells when one of the machine operators gets up from his console and glides over.

"Looks like there's a problem with those new girders, Bill."

Punching the "hold" button on his own computer, Bill goes back to the spacejack's position. Fifteen minutes of fiddling around convinces them both that the first girder from the new pile just is not going to go where it is supposed to go. Using the kind of language that engineers have used since the time of the Egyptians in situations like this, Bill assembles an outside work team. They put on their helmets, get a few extra air canisters from a rack near the airlock, and then shrug themselves into the harnesses attached to their propulsion system—small jets operating on a tank of liquid nitrogen.

When they are suited up, they go out through the airlock and pile into the space cab that brought them from the main shuttle terminal. A short drive brings them to the problem area, halfway out on the new satellite. Coordinating their work with the robot crane operator by radio, they start checking the possible problem points on the girder—a light triangular grid about ten feet on a side and a quarter mile long. After a half hour they finally uncover the problem. The girder, which looks straight to the naked eye, actually has a

To evaluate methods and equipment that might be used in space construction, these astronauts are working in a neutralized gravity tank. Although most of the mundane assembly work in space will probably be done by remote control robots, human construction crews will work outside as well as within control centers.

slight bend to it—enough to keep it from locking into place on the rectangular platform grid. Bill knows that a girder that badly out of shape would never have gotten past the factory inspection system, so he has the crane operator check through the pile of girders off to the side. Sure enough, every one of them is curved.

He reads the serial number off the girder, telling the crane operator to run a check with the central stock computer to see what the problem is. His crew goes back into the space cab and by the time they get back to the main office they have discovered what went wrong. These girders were supposed to be delivered to the construction site for a large space antenna. As far as the computer is concerned, that is where they are, but Bill now knows better.

He puts in a call to John Novak, the chief engineer at the girder fabrication plant. "We've got a problem here, John," he says, and explains that the wrong girders were delivered to his site. While John starts checking around to see what can be done, Bill does the next thing that engineers have always done when faced with inevitable foul-ups of this kind: He tries to find something for the idled crew to do so that precious time is not completely wasted. He puts some men to work cleaning up the various kinds of debris that collects around a construction site, stacking it off to the side where it will be collected and recycled. Two other men begin running structural tests on a recently completed part of the platform— tests that ordinarily would not have to be done for another week, but which might as well be gotten out of the way now.

By the time this new set of jobs is assigned, John Novak is back on the phone. It turns out that the space tug operators who were hauling girders last week simply took the two loads to the wrong places—Bill's girders are at the antenna assembly site, and it will be at least a day before they can be brought over. So now the decision comes down to this: Should he wait until the tugs deliver the new girders, losing a day in the process, or should he send over a small crew to bring a few girders over so that work can get started before quitting time? He decides on the latter course, sends some men with a "space pickup" to get four girders, and takes his morning coffee break. It has been a typical day so far.

Tom Taylor, student

Tom is the last one to leave the apartment in the morning, since he has the shortest distance to go. He does not bother to lock the door, for there is so little crime in the colony. After all, everybody knows everybody else, and they certainly do not have to worry about outsiders. He does not bother waiting for the elevator, but runs down the stairs to the bottom floor of Ventura, where the school complex is located. The first few grades are pretty much like their counterparts on earth, but the eighth grade where Tom goes is like nothing you have ever seen. Each desk is fitted with a computer outlet. Tom sits down at his desk, flips a switch, and says, "French Lesson for Taylor."

The outlet is connected to the central school computer in Vail, and each student's progress in each course is monitored there. The computer knows exactly where Tom left off last time, and picks up from that point. "Bonjour, Monsieur Taylor," it says.

Tom is well into his first-period language lesson by the time the teacher comes around to see how he is doing. They chat for a few moments and the teacher moves on to see if any of the students are having trouble. Only three of the other ten students in the class are studying French, the others having opted for either Russian or Chinese. Twice a week, all of the students studying a particular language go to one of the six schools for a live conversation session. Because of the international nature of the colony, there is no problem getting native speakers of each language to help them get their accents right. And, of course, there are always the television broadcasts from the various countries on earth.

Literature in second period and history in third period are subjects that everyone must take, and today they are spent in class discussions of reading assignments. Tom and his friend Johnny Novak have to go across the colony to "Manhattan" for their physics class that afternoon. When the third-period teacher is not looking, Tom slips a note across to Johnny: "Do you want to walk to Manhattan and eat our lunch on the way?" A quick nod from Johnny, again when the teacher is not looking, sets up the trip. Tom settles down to finish out the history lesson, which is about the ancient Greeks. He has lots of pen pals on earth, and they all think living in the colony must be very exciting. But aside from the occasional field trip to the factory area or the space astronomy lab, Tom really does not see much difference in their schools.

The bell rings and he and Johnny set off to walk the two miles to Manhattan.

Elizabeth Taylor, plant biologist

Ordinarily, Elizabeth would go to her lab in the agricultural building. As director of agricultural research in the colony, she has to oversee a number of operations, including quality control in the hydroponics division, which supplies the colony with all of its fresh vegetables, inspection of incoming material to avoid contamination of the colony, and, most important in her mind, the extensive experimental programs in low- and high-gravity agriculture being carried out in the separate agricultural cylinders around the main colony. But today is special. She has to attend a meeting of all of the colony administrative staff to hear a presentation of plans to build a new cylinder for use as a feedlot for beef animals. This has been debated and discussed in the colony for a long time. It is not at all obvious that the plans to be presented this morning will get the colony any closer to steak dinners, but the political importance of the issue, plus the fact that any new cylinder would undoubtedly involve research programs, have convinced Elizabeth that she should attend personally rather than send her assistant.

She does not have time for the one mile walk to the meeting rooms at "Chicago," so she takes the elevator to the central hub, experiencing her only weightless period of the day. Descending on the Chicago elevator, she sees Vince Gennario, director of space construction. She smiles. "I see they roped you into this, too."

"Well," says Vince, "if they're going to tell me to build this thing, I guess I'd better be here to make sure they don't ask me to do something impossible."

The presentation is in one of the large meeting rooms in the lower level of the "public space" section of Chicago. The colony mayor opens the session with a short summary of the history of the idea of a space feedlot operation for beef. A recent arrival from the engineering planning section of Vince Gennario's operation explains further, complete with crisp blueprints and detailed completion schedules for the construction of the new cylinder. Elizabeth smiles. She can not help but compare the neat design on the slides with the stories about spacejacking that she hears from Bill. She wishes the newcomer good luck.

Elizabeth's boss, the head of the colony food supply system, outlines the general operation. Several cows, suitably sedated, along with a few heifers will be brought up on a shuttle flight. There is no need for a bull, of course, since breeding of choice cattle is usually done by artificial insemination anyway. With careful breeding and attention, the goal of one steak dinner a month for every colonist should be met within five years.

The final presentation, by the colony's financial officer, is pretty boring. During the discussion period that follows, Elizabeth makes sure that the planners have left enough space and facilities for her research group in the new cylinder, and the meeting breaks up. She has a quick lunch in the Chicago cafeteria and heads back to her office. She wants to have a short afternoon staff meeting and get her desk cleared before she goes home.

Evening at the Taylors'

Bill is the first one home that evening. It is his turn to make supper, so when he gets home he puts together the ingredients for his famous rabbit stew and sets them on the stove to simmer. By this time Elizabeth has come back from the hydroponic building and Tom has called to say that he will be home late because the Little League Space Polo team has an extra practice. With over an hour of free time before dinner is ready, Bill and Elizabeth put on their jogging suits and take the elevator to ground level. They both belong to the "Four-Mile Club" in the colony, and they like to run the jogging path around the entire rim several times a week to stay in shape and to keep their membership current. It is an odd-numbered day, so all of the traffic on the jogging path is moving "clockwise." They set out at an easy pace, but by the time they reach the three-mile mark with their home apartment complex almost coming into view ahead, Bill is puffing. The fact that he spends so much of his time in free fall means that his muscles are not as accustomed to the strain of gravity as are Elizabeth's. It is quite common, in fact, for space workers to have to exercise more than their counterparts who stay in the colony in order to keep in shape. Elizabeth slows her pace a little to accommodate Bill, and they finish the final stretch together.

A quick navy-style shower for each of them and it is time for dinner. Tom returns from his practice and disappears into the shower while Bill pours two glasses of rose petal wine. The wine is brewed by one of their neighbors by processes that home winemakers have used for centuries, and Bill always trades some of his artichokes for it. Alcoholic beverages, of course, can not be brought up from earth, so old-fashioned home brewing has become an interesting and profitable hobby for some members of the colony. Then Tom joins the family and they sit down to dinner on their patio.

The first course is a lettuce and tomato salad, using products that were under Elizabeth's care in the hydroponic building a few days earlier. Bill's rabbit stew is the main course, followed by ice cream for dessert. The dinner dishes are then put next to those from breakfast in the dishwasher, and the ultrasound appliance starts through its cleaning cycle. Water, of course, is much too valuable to be used for a job like dishwashing.

What to do for the evening? It being a weekday, Tom has homework, so he returns to his room, puts on his stereo headset, and starts to study. How he can study that way is beyond his parents, as it is beyond their earthbound counterparts. Bill and Elizabeth look at the home computer printout of the evening's events. Let's see . . . a chamber music concert over in Vail, a space polo game in the hub, a widescreen showing of *Carmen* live from the La Scala Opera House in Milan in the theater on the ground floor of their own building, and a first-run movie at Vail.

Nothing really appeals, so they decide to spend a quiet

evening at home. Bill picks up the computer printout of the novel he started a few days ago—a novel in which the romantic life of the spacejack is portrayed in glowing terms. It should be good for a laugh after a day like today. Elizabeth decides to catch up on some of the professional journals that she needs to follow, so she instructs the computer to display the list of articles available. Scanning the list, she comes across one that looks interesting, so she has the article displayed on the screen. After reading a few paragraphs she decides that this is something she should look into in more detail, so she punches in instructions for the computer to produce a hard copy for her. A minute later five sheets of paper slide out at the bottom of the machine, and she takes them and settles down to read. When she finishes the article, she will decide whether it is important enough to keep on file or whether she just needs to make a note of where she found it and return the paper to the machine for recyling. Time enough for that later.

At ten o'clock, she and Bill turn on the home television and Tom joins them to watch the news. The program is produced on earth and beamed up to the colony, and it is not too different from the national network news broadcasts shown in the United States. The only difference is that there are no commercials—who on the colony would buy a car, anyway? After the international news, a short summary of colony news comes on. This would be pretty dull stuff for anyone on earth, of course, but people in the colony, like people in any small town, like to keep up with what is going on locally, what clubs are meeting, what the local politicians are up to, and so on. This section of the news also contains information about ship dockings and the status of various projects in the colony. The one occupying center stage right now is the proposal to build the agricultural cylinder for raising beef. Old earthsiders like Bill and Elizabeth are much in favor of this move—the occasional beefsteak they can get does not really satisfy their taste for the meat they grew up with. Younger people like Tom do not see what all the fuss is about. What's the matter with rabbit and lamb, anyway? So the debate goes on, as political debates always do.

Meanwhile, outside the colony the huge mirrors are starting to swing to a new alignment, and "night" falls. The Taylor family goes to bed. Thinking about the novel he has just finished, Bill turns to his wife and says, "I wonder why people on earth think life on the colony is so different and exciting?"

PART III: AFTER THE FIRST COLONY

11 | Our Long-Range Future in Space

In the short term, the most likely economic activity in space would be the generation of power for an energy-starved world. We would not, however, expect this to remain true beyond the first generation of space colonists. For one thing, there is a limit to the number of people who can live on earth, even with abundant power, and therefore a limit to how much power they will need. Furthermore, there are probably also limits to the amount of energy that can be transferred to the earth from space without seriously upsetting the climate. For example, if we ever started using power satellites to beam an amount of energy to the earth that is comparable to what we get from the sun, it would be impossible to avoid heating the atmosphere. Scientists have imagined scenarios in which such trends get out of hand and turn the earth into a copy of the planet Venus, with eternal clouds and temperatures high above the boiling point of water.

In Chapter 5 we discuss another possible activity in space: the mining of asteroids for raw materials. In the long run, this particular resource is sure to be more important than sunlight, if for no other reason than that it will allow the construction of more and more homes for human beings in space at a time when room on the surface of the mother planet is becoming more and more difficult to find. It is inevitable that once the colonies are a going concern, attention will be turned from lunar- to deep-space mining.

When any large planetary body is formed, there is a period when the heat generated by meteors falling on the growing planet is enough to melt the entire structure. During this molten period, most of the heavy materials in the body tend to sink toward the center. This is why the core of the earth is largely made of iron. Only small amounts of the heavier materials are left near the surface when the planet cools off. These "leftovers" are what are sought for so avidly in mining on earth today.

But if you think about it for a moment, you will see that the process of forming a large, planet-sized body is nothing more than a way of taking metals from a place where they are relatively accessible—in small asteroids—and putting them deep into the interior of a planet. In fact, when you come right down to it, the surface of a planet is the last place you would look for minerals if you had a choice. Your chances of success would be much higher if you could go back to the place where the minerals came from in the first place . . . to the asteroid itself.

We all know that there is a large belt of asteroids between the orbits of Mars and Jupiter. At one time it was thought that they constituted the remains of a planet that exploded early in the history of the solar system—an idea that we might call the "Krypton" hypothesis. Actually, the evidence now points to the idea that these asteroids are the ingredients of a planet that never formed. As such, they constitute just the sort of unseparated source of heavy minerals that we were discussing above. They are, in effect, the richest and most easily accessible source of such materials in the solar system.

Occasionally, a traffic accident occurs in the asteroid belt.

Sometimes two asteroids collide with each other, or a passing comet causes an asteroid to leave its original orbit. When this happens, it is possible that the asteroid that is knocked out of the belt will go into an orbit that brings it inside the orbit of the earth. Such bodies are called Apollo asteroids. Their orbits are illustrated in figure 12. They tend to be small bodies, anywhere from a few hundred yards to a few miles across; consequently, it is only very recently that astronomers have studied them seriously. Nevertheless, we know now that many such asteroids exist. Because they are closer to the earth than are bodies in the asteroid belt, Apollo objects are the first place we would look if we were seriously considering space mining.

Figure 12

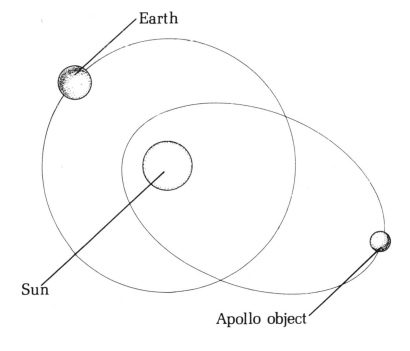

Actually, we can make a pretty good guess as to the extent of the resources available in Apollo asteroids, since meteorites—stones that fall from the heavens—can be analyzed on the earth right now. Presumably, their chemical composition is similar to that of the asteroids that occur in regions of space near the earth. A few years ago a colleague of mine at the University of Virginia, astrophysicist Robert Rood, and I looked at this problem. We started by taking the known chemical composition of meteorites and assuming that Apollo asteroids have the same percentage of each mineral. We then looked up the expected demand for a number of scarce minerals for the year 2000 AD. Finally, we asked how much of this demand would be met if a single asteroid about six miles on a side were to be mined. The results were very interesting, as you can see by inspecting the table on the next page.

This table has to be taken with a grain of salt, since it would not necessarily be economical to take an asteroid apart atom by atom to recover its mineral content, any more than we take a mountain apart that way to recover iron or silver. The point is that the resources of space—even of a few asteroids—are huge compared to the rate at which we now consume those resources. Literally everything we need is waiting for us a few hundred miles up.

In addition, there is one class of asteroids that goes by the horrible-sounding name of carbonaceous chondrites that is particularly interesting from the point of view of space colonies. These asteroids are known to have reasonably high concentrations of organic materials in them, and organic materials are rich in hydrogen, the most precious element in near-earth space. The first asteroids mined may be of this type, and the most important result of the mining from the point of view of the colonists may well be that their store of hydrogen may, for the first time, make the space colonies

Amount of critical minerals in an asteroid 10 km. on a side

mineral	amount in asteroid	number of years the amount will last at consumption rates for the year 2000 AD
aluminum	1.5×11^{11} tons	23,000
chromium	1.2×10^{10} tons	22,000
copper	3.0×10^5 tons	14
gold	6.0×10^7 tons	30,000
lead	3.0×10^6 tons	0.5
manganese	3.0×10^9 tons	1,360
mercury	7.9×10^7 flasks*	294
molybdenum	3.0×10^6 tons	10
silver	3.5×10^5 tons	19
tin	3.0×10^7 tons	97
tungsten	3.0×10^5 tons	4
zinc	3.0×10^8 tons	24

* 1 flask = 76 pounds

independent of earth as far as their water supply is concerned.

The actual problem of tapping the resources of an Apollo asteroid is primarily one of changing the orbit of the asteroid so that it floats along with the colony's space manufacturing facility. The mining process could then proceed and the unused portions of the asteroid would probably be incorporated into radiation shields for various structures.

The actual orbit change could be accomplished in a number of ways. The most straightforward would be to tow a small solar power satellite to the asteroid and use it to power a mass driver. The mass driver in this case, unlike its counterpart on the moon, would not be used to move material into space, but rather to propel the asteroid itself. Every time a pellet left the mass driver, the asteroid would recoil a little. The steady pushing caused by a stream of pellets being thrown into space would effect the desired change in orbit.

This would be a slow process, of course. Some plans call for a period of several years during which the asteroid would be moved into its new position. Presumably the crews would be changed every year when the asteroid came near the colony. Probably the mining of the richest lodes of ore would take place during this period as well, leaving the harder extractions for the time when the asteroid could get the full attention of the colony's work crews.

Other ways of moving asteroids around have been proposed. Cliff Singer of Princeton University has proposed placing a column of debris in the path of an asteroid to slow it down and bring it into a new orbit. Ken Brown, a student at the University of Virginia, and I have done some calculations that indicate that under certain circumstances it might be easy to nudge one asteroid and cause it to collide with another. In this scheme, the second asteroid then moves into the desired orbit as a result of the collision. If this turned out to be a useful way of doing things, asteroid mining would become something like a giant game of celestial billiards.

In any case, there seems little doubt that it will be technically feasible to tap the mineral resources of the Apollo asteroids once the space colony and its manufacturing systems are in place. This, in turn, will open up an entire new era in human development. The energy resources that we have from the sun and from minerals are so large by present standards that we might as well think of them as being unlimited, even if they are not completely so.

It seems likely that the first response to this development will be a spurt in the building of space colonies. With manufacturing facilities already in place and with both lunar and asteroid mining going full blast, there is no reason to expect

In this artist's concept, a small transportation vehicle waits for lift-off from a lunar mining town. Lunar materials will be the prime resources for the metals and oxygen for a space colony. Once a colony is established, full-scale mining of other planetary bodies such as asteroids will be possible.

that the Stanford Torus, which we discussed in the first chapter of the book, will remain the best possible habitat design. Improved building techniques and an abundant resource base will make it possible to build colonies several miles across, providing homes for hundreds of thousands of people at a time. Before too long, we can imagine that the earth-moon region will be liberally sprinkled with these colonies, and that people will start to look elsewhere for locations.

Since by this time there will be third- and fourth-generation space dwellers, the idea of returning to a planetary surface probably will not seem very attractive. Life in the colony, with its controlled environment and attractive design, will seem much more desirable than a return to earth or pioneering on another planet, such as Mars. In point of fact, it seems pretty reasonable to suppose that the primary concern of people choosing sites for new colonies will not be proximity to earth, but proximity to raw materials, especially since energy in the form of sunlight is pretty well universally available in the solar system. And locating the new colony near sources of raw materials pretty well guarantees that they will be in the outer solar system—either in the asteroid belt or near one of the large planets.

To understand why the first "new" colonies will be built so far from earth, we have to remember that in space distance is not equivalent to energy. This is not true on earth, where driving your car twice a given distance will use up twice as much gas. In space, once the energy necessary to get an object moving has been expended, the object will keep on moving forever. This means that if miners get an asteroid moving on the right course, it will eventually wind up at the space manufacturing center near earth. No special propulsion will be required, other than an occasional in-course correction. It makes no difference if the process started in the asteroid belt, the rings of Saturn, or the moons of Jupiter.

In Chapter 3 we introduced the concept of the energy tax, or the energy required to lift a pound of material from the surface of the earth to a given orbit. We recall that it cost roughly eight kilowatt-hours of energy to lift a pound from the surface of the earth to free space. In the table below we give the energy tax required to move a pound of material from the earth's orbit to various other parts of the solar system. Although these energy taxes are larger than those associated with climbing up from the surface of the earth, the energy needed to change an orbit can be applied over a long period of time. This means that even relatively small rockets working over long periods can do the job. In the case of course changes done by mass drivers, of course, the energy will come from the sun and no conventional fuel would be needed at all. The most important thing to see in the table is that the extra energy tax imposed by moving from the asteroid belt to any of the other planets is a small percentage of the total tax.

Actually, some writers have suggested that the first site for colonies away from the earth will not be the asteroid belt, but the rings of Saturn. The reason for this argument has to do with one of the central facts of the near-earth environment: the lack of hydrogen and/or water. We know that part of the rings of Saturn are made up of chunks of ice several miles on a side. Mining just one such spaceborne glacier would provide enough water for hundreds of space colonies, and there is virtually an endless supply of them near Saturn. So once the space colony movement gets away from the earth-moon system, the constraint imposed by the necessity of importing hydrogen from earth will disappear, and with it the last real limitation on human expansion into space.

Whether the first distant colony will be one housing hardrock miners in the asteroid belt or ice miners near Saturn, the energy tax arguments we made earlier give us a pretty good idea of how the transportation system that brings their products back home will work. We can think of the

Energy tax for movement from the earth's orbit	
other points in the solar system	
destination	*tax (kw-hr)*
Mars	19.4
asteroid belt	39.5
Jupiter	45.3
Saturn	50.4
Pluto	54.8

connection as sort of a pipeline. The miners will start their products—either raw asteroids or partially refined ores or maybe just chunks of ice—moving in the direction of their ultimate destination. The journey for a given object may take many months or even years. Once the operation has been going for a while, though, this time lag will not matter. The space manufacturing center will receive a steady supply of material, and whatever flows out of that end of the pipeline will be replaced at the other end.

In a similar vein, the distant colonies need to be no more isolated from the culture of earth than the original torus was. The only difference between sending a television signal to a colony orbiting the earth and one orbiting Saturn is that the latter take longer to reach its destination. No one actually watching the broadcast could tell that it was not live. So all of the remarks we made about the level of cultural activity on the torus would continue to hold for a colony anywhere in the solar system. In fact, it is likely that as the number of colonies grows there will be an electronic web linking all of them with each other and with earth, creating a truly system-wide culture in which the mother planet will play an important, but not necessarily dominant, part. In this respect, earth may well play the role for the expanding space civilization that Europe did for the United States in the nineteenth century. It will serve as a source of history, of cultural forms, and as a center of education during the period that the colonies are developing their own unique cultures.

How long it would take for the human race to expand throughout the entire solar system is a matter of conjecture. Most authors give estimates in the range of two hundred to four hundred years, a time scale that seems reasonable to me. Given the fact that a colony, once established, can be almost completely self-sufficient, there is no particular restriction on where in the solar system the colonies will be located. Provided they are not in the shadow of another colony—a pretty unlikely event, given the vast extent of the available space—there will always be solar energy to run the colony. In fact, Gerard O'Neill has worked out what may be the only fundamental limitation on colony location. He asked how far away from the sun a colony would have to be before the mass of its solar collectors would become equal to the mass of the colony itself. It turns out that this would happen someplace well outside the orbit of Pluto. Consequently, we can state with some confidence that even the remotest reaches of our solar system could be populated by human beings living in space colonies. Whether they *will* be, of course, is another question. Even on earth, the fact that people could live in Antarctica does not mean that they will do so in large numbers.

But in any case, it seems reasonable to suppose that the quest for raw materials to feed a growing space industry will eventually cause human beings to populate many parts of our solar system that now seem remote. And lest the idea that mining asteroids might be an important human activity in the future seems farfetched to you, consider the following fact: During the 1960s about half of the earth's supply of nickel came from a deposit in Ontario known as the Sudbury Astrobleme. This is the remains of a meteor that struck the earth long ago. So the next time you spend a 1965 nickel, you may be using material that was, in fact, mined from an asteroid!

12 | The Final Frontier

Perhaps the most important aspect of the space colony idea is that it shows that the future of the human race need not be tied to the availability of planetary surfaces on which human beings can survive. This is fortunate, because we have reason to believe that earth-type planets are rather rare in the universe. Certainly this is true in our own solar system. If we have learned anything from the planetary exploration program that NASA has carried out over the last decade, it is that there is nowhere in the solar system, other than our own earth, where life of any kind can exist. This means that wherever the human race decides to go in the next few centuries, it will have to take its own environment with it.

The choice, then, will be between two options: Either we will build equivalent life-support systems on the surfaces of some of the planets, or we will build colonies in space, outside of the gravitational well of any planet. In all likelihood we will do both.

Colonization of Other Planets

There will surely be underground or domed cities on the moon and Mars within a hundred years. Many of the problems we have discussed for the space colony—recycling of resources, scarcity of some materials such as water, protecting humans from a lethal outside environment—will have to be solved for these ground-based dwellings. In addition, any commerce between the planet- or moon-based colony and the earth will have to pay an extra energy tax on every shipment made, over and above that associated with getting off of the surface of the earth.

Even if it were felt worthwhile to pay this extra energy tax, there are only two bodies in the solar system—Venus and Mars—that provide a gravity near that of the earth. Since we decided in Chapter 1 that earth-normal gravity was one of the essential features that would have to exist in any long-term human environment, this fact immediately eliminates most planetary surface area from consideration for colonization. In addition, the extreme conditions on the surface of Venus (temperatures above eight hundred degrees, sulphuric acid rain, and so on) make it unlikely that anything other than research outposts will ever be established there.

Thus, in our system only Mars, and possibly the moon if the gravity requirement is relaxed somewhat, can be expected to serve as homes for the human race. This fact is in stark contrast to the science-fiction of only a few decades ago, which dealt with Venus as a sort of watery version of a tropical swamp and Mars as an arid desert with canals and a breathable atmosphere. A quick survey of the solar system, then, shows that we might as well build our own "real estate" in the form of colonies, since very little of the natural surfaces around seem to be suitable, or even adaptable, to our needs.

Actually, as we mentioned above, the appearance of earth-type planets—that is, planets where liquid water exists on the surface over long periods of time—is expected to be rather rare. The earth itself has been treading a rather narrow path throughout its 4.5 billion-year history between twin disasters. Had it been a little closer to the sun, more water would have evaporated from the oceans, and the ability of the oceans to absorb the carbon dioxide thrown into the atmosphere by volcanoes would have been diminished. The extra carbon dioxide in the atmosphere would have reflected some of the heat that is now radiated into space, causing the earth to warm up. This warming, in turn, would lead to a still greater evaporation in the oceans, more carbon dioxide in the atmosphere, and yet higher temperatures. This process, called a "runaway greenhouse effect," would eventually result in the creation of a world much like Venus. It has been estimated that if the earth had been 5 percent closer to the sun than it is, this would have been its fate.

On the other hand, if the earth were farther from the sun than it is, the winters would be longer. Since snow reflects sunlight back into space more efficiently than ground, less of the sun's heat would remain to warm the atmosphere. This would cause the next winter to be colder, with more snow staying on the ground a longer time and reflecting even more sunlight, which, in turn, would make the temperature lower still. The final effect of this sort of "runaway glaciation" is a world in which almost all of the water is frozen and no life forms capable of putting oxygen into the atmosphere can develop. If the earth had been 1 percent farther away from the sun than it is, this would have been its fate.

So there is, in fact, a very narrow zone around the sun in which a planet capable of supporting human life could be found. The same kinds of calculations indicate that only stars similar to the sun have such zones at all. Consequently, we can expect that the average planetary system will have no earth-type planets, and that the occurrence of such planets in the universe will be quite rare.

From this discussion we can draw two important conclusions:

1. Surface colonization within the solar system is likely to be limited to Mars and perhaps one or two moons.
2. There is little probability that earth-type planets will be found abundantly anywhere else in the galaxy.

Interstellar Travel and Space Colonies

We saw in Chapter 11 that most of the recoverable mineral resources in the solar system are located in the asteroid belt and near the outer planets. For this reason alone we would expect that space colonies of the type we have been discussing will be built, whether or not a parallel effort toward colonizing the few available surfaces is made. And given the tendency of all living systems—the human race included—to fill every space that it can, we can also expect that in a few centuries the attractive spots in the solar system will be pretty well filled up with clusters of O'Neill colonies. At that point the human race will face an important choice: Either we will opt for some solar-system-wide version of zero population growth, or we will seek our future in the stars. I like to think that we will choose the latter course, and that the existence of space colonies is what will make it possible.

If we are going to talk about interstellar travel, though, we had better get a few facts firmly in mind. The most important one is the fact that the distances involved are so large that they are hard to picture. An analogy will help us make this point. Suppose the sun were reduced in size to something the size of a small watermelon, a foot across the middle. Suppose we placed this shrunken sun in the middle of New York City and started walking away from it. When we had traveled about ten steps (thirty feet), we would see a small grain of

This artist's concept of the exterior of a space colony reflected in an astronaut's helmet symbolizes the exciting possibilities of man's existence in space.

dust. This would be the planet Mercury, the closest planet to the sun. When we had walked a little over thirty yards, still much less than a city block, we would see a small sphere about as big across as a nail. This would be the earth.

If we kept walking, we would pass the other members of

the solar system until, about a mile from our starting point, we would encounter Pluto, the outermost planet. If we then wanted to go to the nearest star, Alpha Centauri, we would have to walk all the way to the Pacific Ocean and travel (presumably by boat) to Hawaii. And this would take us to a star whose distance from our own is 4.4 light-years.

If you recall that the planetary probes we send from earth take months and even years to get to the outer planets, you realize immediately that the immense empty spaces between stars mean that totally new means of transportation will have to be devised if the human race is ever to leave the solar system. For example, an object traveling at the speed of seven miles per second, fast enough to escape from the earth's gravitational influence, would require no less than 117,000 years to get to Alpha Centauri—far too long for there to be any reasonable hope of having a living system survive the trip. Even starships capable of traveling at 10 percent of the speed of light would, when the acceleration and deceleration times are taken into account, require over a hundred years to get there. It is obvious from these remarks that the kind of interstellar travel one encounters in science-fiction novels, with individuals flitting from one star to another in a matter of weeks or months, will not be possible unless some entirely new laws of physics are discovered.

So long as we talk about starships built to operate according to the laws of physics that we now know, it is impossible to make even a one-way trip between stars in less than a human lifetime. This has led some well-known scientists to conclude that interstellar travel is simply impossible. But once we understand that it is possible to recreate earthlike conditions in the man-made environment of the space colony, this objection to interstellar travel becomes somewhat pointless. After all, if you happen to be a fifth-generation space colonist, and if neither you nor your parents nor your grandparents have ever set foot on the surface of a planet, would it make much difference to you if your colony were orbiting the sun or on a journey to Alpha Centauri?

Think of this question another way. Since you started reading this chapter, the earth has traveled over five thousand miles in its annual journey around the sun. Assuming that you were aware of this fact, would it matter to you? In just the same way, we can expect that residents of a moving version of the space colony will not mind if their "home" moves through space at 10 percent of the speed of light.

Once we accept the fact that a few generations from now human beings will be used to living in a totally man-made environment, then the idea of a journey of 150 years does not seem all that farfetched. It simply would mean that the great-grandchildren of the adults who started the trip would be the ones to see the destination. But since we have seen that a colony could be self-sustaining for this long a period, and since the everyday operation of the colony would occupy the attention of the travelers, it does not seem at all unreasonable that this future version of Noah's Ark would reach its destination with the human inhabitants alive and well.

There are literally dozens of designs of propulsion systems for starships that have been suggested to date. All of them use techniques that are either available now or that can reasonably be expected to be available within a few decades. One of these, proposed by physicist Freeman Dyson and called "Project Orion," uses a string of small hydrogen bombs exploded in back of the ship to provide the motive power. Another, suggested by physicist Cliff Singer, moves the ship by shooting baseball-sized pellets at it from a large mass driver anchored in the asteroid belt. There is little doubt that at least one of the designs already suggested will be found to be a practical way of running a starship, and it is not too much to expect that additional suggestions will be made in the new few centuries. It is a pretty safe bet that when the time comes when people want to build vessels capable of going to nearby stars, they will have techniques available to do so.

The voyagers would find themselves living in a structure not unlike the ones in which they grew up. If the flight plan called for the ship to accelerate until it reached the midpoint of its course and then decelerate the rest of the way, then the pseudogravity would not have to be supplied by rotation. The acceleration itself would provide the sensation of weight in much the same way as an upward-accelerating elevator makes you feel as if you are being pulled into the floor. Everything else about the ship would be familiar—the air and water recycling systems, the agricultural plant, the individual homes built from asteroid materials. The new occupants would feel no stranger in their new home than modern Americans would if they moved from St. Louis to Denver. They might, in fact, like their new situation better than what they had had, because one of the planning requirements of a multigenerational ship would surely be the provision of space so that there could be more people at the end of the journey than there were at the beginning.

The starfarers would not be sent out at random, of course. Small unmanned probes would have explored the system to which they were being sent, and they would have a pretty good idea of what to expect when they got there. They would need energy, which would be available in the form of light from their new star, and they would need materials. Presumably they would head for something like the asteroid belt, where these could be gathered without much trouble. Exploring and populating the planets in the new system would be a very low priority on their list. In good time, the new system would fill up with new O'Neill colonies. Eventually it, too, would send out probes and starships to still more distant systems. The web of stars surrounded by humans living in space colonies would continue to grow and expand.

So we see that when the first space colony is built near the earth, more will have been done than simply providing an exotic new environment for a few adventurous individuals. The human race will have taken its first step on the road to a future in which the entire galaxy, not just one small planet, will be our home.

Index